Nestle is a pivotal entity in the global food industry. This case study examines the factors behind Nestlé's enduring success, highlighting key milestones, strategic decisions, and the cultural ethos that defines its operations worldwide. It offers a comprehensive view of how Nestlé has navigated challenges and capitalized on opportunities, setting benchmarks for excellence in the global marketplace.

Acknowledgements

I am deeply grateful for the invaluable support and guidance of my family, mentors, and friends throughout my study of Nestlé. Their hands-on experience and insightful perspectives have enriched this case study immeasurably.

The expertise of my mentors has been instrumental in navigating the complexities of Nestlé's history and operations.The support of my friends and family has been invaluable in shaping the narrative of this study.

This case study stands as a testament to the collaborative effort of those who have shared their knowledge and insights into Nestlé. I am privileged to have had such a supportive network throughout this journey.

Introduction

Nestlé, originating from Switzerland, stands as the foremost global entity in the fields of nutrition, health, and wellness, as well as being the largest food corporation based on sales figures. Their extensive range of products includes baby food, breakfast cereals, coffee, confectionery, dairy items, frozen foods, pet food, yogurt, and snacks, featuring well-known brands such as Stouffers, Nescafe, Kit-Kat, Carnation, and Nestlé Water.

With a longstanding commitment to sourcing top-tier raw materials for their products, Nestlé has consistently surpassed its competitors, leading to significant market growth. This dedication to quality traces back to its Swiss origins and its inception in 1866 by Henri Nestlé, originally known as the Anglo-Swiss Condensed Milk Company. Over the years, Nestlé's influence in the food industry has been undeniable, earning them placements on prestigious lists like Forbes and the Fortune 500.

Mission, Vision and Core Values

Mission Statement

According to Nestlé's mission statement, the company aims to be recognized as the world's leading provider of nutrition, health, and wellness products. Their commitment to the motto "Good Food, Good Life" underscores their dedication to offering customers the highest quality and most nutritious options across various food and beverage categories and consumption occasions.

Nestlé, headquartered in Switzerland, is renowned as the foremost nutrition, health, and wellness company globally and holds the top position in food sales. Their product portfolio encompasses a wide range of items including baby food, breakfast cereals, coffee, confectionery, dairy products, frozen food, pet food, yogurt, and snacks. Notable brands under the Nestlé umbrella include Stouffers, Nescafe, Kit-Kat, Nestlé Water, among others.

The mission statement's emphasis on providing a diverse selection of food and beverage categories highlights Nestlé's commitment to catering to the varied needs and preferences of consumers.

Nestlé's success can largely be attributed to its extensive range of health-oriented products, as outlined in its mission statement. Additionally, the company's dedication to continuous innovation and product line expansion plays a crucial role in driving its achievements.

Vision Statement

Nestlé's vision statement aims to establish itself as a global leader in the fields of nutrition, healthcare, and wellness while delivering enhanced value to shareholders. The statement emphasizes the company's commitment to being a preferred employer, partner, and provider of products and services.

The intriguing aspect of the vision statement lies in its focus on shareholder value and being the preferred choice in the business landscape. The interconnectedness between these two aspects suggests that Nestlé seeks to achieve market dominance by prioritizing its role as an employer and provider. By excelling in these areas, the company ensures profitability and success for its shareholders.

In essence, Nestlé's primary objective appears to be achieving profitability while simultaneously positioning itself as the preferred choice in the market.

Core Values

"Full legal conformity, integrity, fair dealings, integrity, and respect" are Nestlé's basic principles.

Nestlé's core principles revolve around upholding legal compliance, integrity, fairness, respect, and honesty. These principles aim to establish Nestlé as a reputable and trustworthy organization. By embodying these values, Nestlé can expand into new markets and evolve into a leading global corporation. These principles are ingrained in Nestlé's organizational culture, ensuring that all employees worldwide adhere to ethical standards and established procedures. Furthermore, they emphasize the importance of fostering positive relationships and interdependencies among various stakeholders.

The food and beverage industry is experiencing rapid growth, driven by the essential nature of food consumption for human survival. This industry encompasses a diverse array of businesses worldwide, collectively supplying the majority of the world's food. Intense competition within this industry necessitates continuous improvement and innovation across various aspects of business operations, including product development and cost reduction efforts. Despite facing challenges such as economic fluctuations and price volatility, the global food and beverage industry remains resilient and continues to expand steadily.

According to a report from Plunkett Research, the global food and beverage industry contributes significantly to the world's GDP, accounting for over 10% and exceeding US$ 8 trillion in value. Despite economic challenges in certain markets, the industry maintains its growth trajectory, driven by major players like Nestlé, Anheuser-Busch InBev, and PepsiCo.

Nestlé, ranked as the second largest food and beverage company globally in the Forbes Global 2000 list, has been surpassed by Anheuser-Busch InBev, which now holds the top position. Despite this shift, Nestlé remains a key player in the industry. PepsiCo also holds a prominent position, ranking third in the food and beverage category, showcasing the competitive landscape and dominance of major corporations in this sector.

3.1. CHALLENGES OF THE FOOD AND BEVERAGE INDUSTRY

The food and beverage industry has undergone significant transformations in recent years, driven by shifting consumer preferences and ongoing innovation within the sector. These changes have presented both opportunities and challenges for industry players. One of the primary challenges is meeting the evolving demands of consumers who are increasingly focused on nutrition and health. This includes preferences for products that are low in fat and offer nutritional benefits. As a result, companies like Nestlé must not only prioritize product quality but also ensure that their offerings align with nutritional standards and cater to health-conscious consumers.

Additionally, challenges related to raw material quality and product traceability have emerged as important considerations for food and beverage companies. Ensuring the integrity and safety of ingredients throughout the supply chain is essential for maintaining consumer trust and compliance with regulatory requirements. Nestlé, like other industry players, faces the task of addressing these challenges to uphold the quality and safety of its products.

In response to these challenges, Nestlé is focusing on developing new and innovative products that appeal to consumers' changing preferences while also enhancing the quality of its existing offerings. By doing so, the company aims to strengthen its reputation and competitive position in the market. Ultimately, Nestlé's business model is evolving to address these challenges and adapt to the changing landscape of the food and beverage industry, with a renewed emphasis on innovation, quality, and consumer health.

3.2. SALES EVOLUTION OF THE INDUSTRY

The Food & Beverage industry occupies a significant position within the consumer segment, contributing substantially to overall sales and revenues. One of the key factors contributing to its appeal for investors is its non-cyclical nature, primarily driven by the essential nature of its products. Unlike industries that may experience fluctuations in demand based on economic conditions or consumer sentiment, the demand for food and beverages remains relatively stable regardless of the prevailing financial situation or economic performance.

This stability is attributed to the fact that food and beverages are basic necessities, essential for sustaining life, and fulfilling fundamental human needs. As a result, consumers continue to purchase these products regardless of economic downturns or fluctuations in disposable income. This consistent demand creates a reliable revenue stream for companies operating within the industry, making it an attractive investment option for investors seeking stability and steady returns.

The graph provided illustrates the evolution of sales within the industry over time, demonstrating a pattern of steady growth and stability. Despite fluctuations in various economic indicators or external factors, the sales trajectory of the Food & Beverage industry has remained relatively consistent, indicating its resilience and enduring appeal to consumers. This consistent performance further reinforces the industry's attractiveness to investors, as it offers the potential for sustainable growth and returns over the long term.

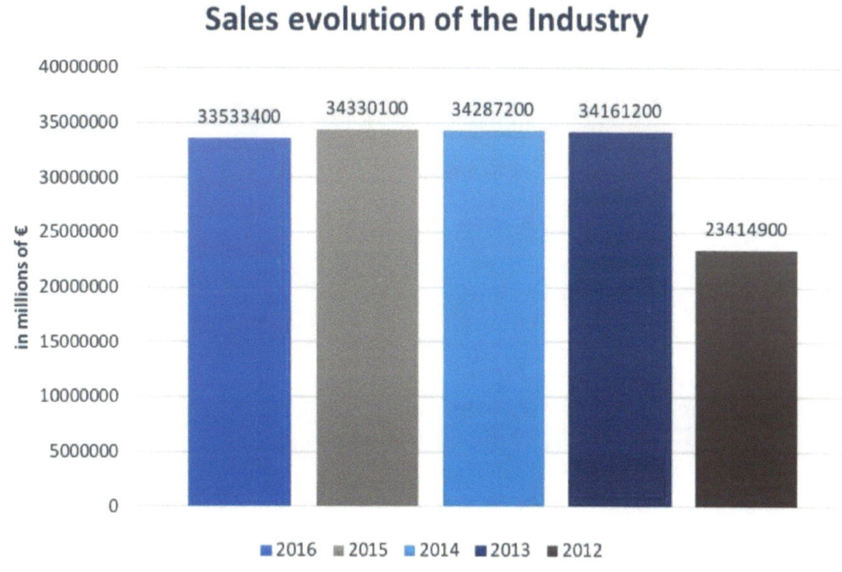

Figure 2: Sales evolution of the industry.
Source: Amadeus

The figures provided (Figures 3 and 4) depict the expected growth of sales and revenues within the Food & Beverage industry. In 2018, the total revenue reached 84.743 million Euros, reflecting a significant revenue growth rate of 16.6% compared to the previous period. This substantial increase in revenue indicates strong performance and positive momentum within the industry during that year.

Looking ahead, the graphs suggest that total revenues are projected to continue growing in the coming years. This anticipated growth trajectory underscores the industry's resilience and ongoing demand for food and beverage products. Factors such as population growth, changing consumer preferences, and evolving dietary trends contribute to this sustained growth outlook.

However, it's noteworthy that while total revenues are expected to continue increasing, the growth rate is forecasted to decrease over time. This implies that while the industry will continue to expand, the pace of growth may gradually moderate in the future. Several factors could contribute to this slowdown in growth, including market saturation, increased competition, and economic factors affecting consumer spending patterns.

Despite the projected decrease in the growth rate, the Food & Beverage industry remains a robust and essential sector of the economy, offering opportunities for investment and continued revenue generation. Companies operating within this industry will need to adapt to changing market dynamics and consumer preferences to maintain their competitive edge and sustain growth in the long term.

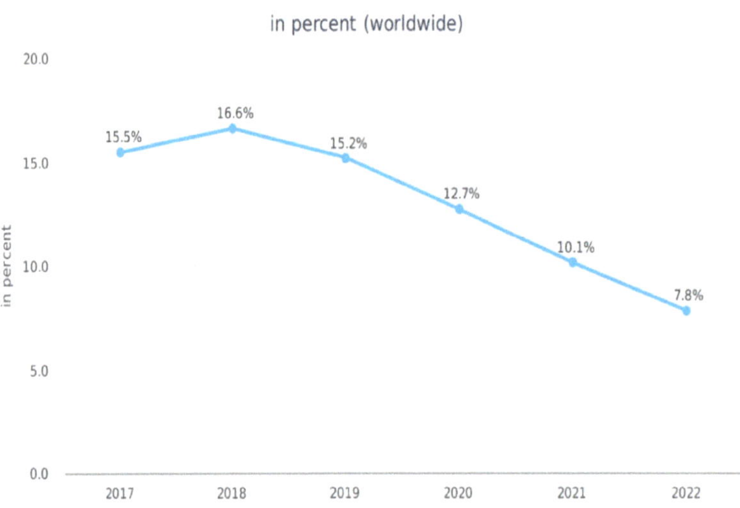

Figure 3: Revenue Growth in the food and beverage market (in percent).
Source: Statista, September 2018; Selected region only includes countries listed in the Digital Market Outlook Outlook.

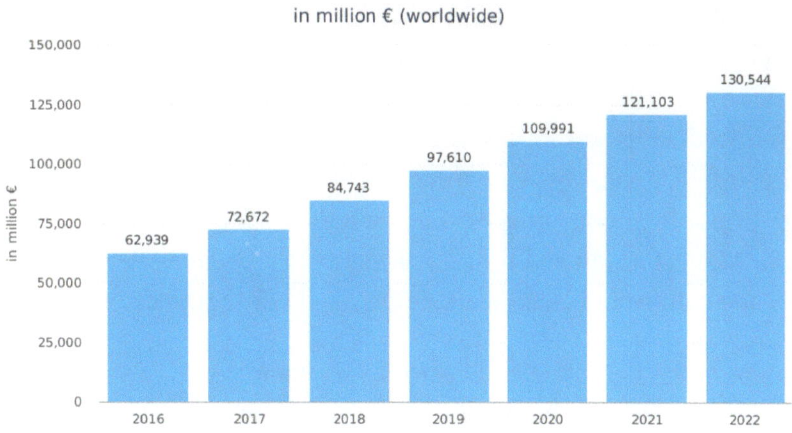

Figure 4: Revenue in the Food & beverage market (in million €).
Source: Statista, September 2018; Selected region only includes countries listed in the Digital Market Outlook Outlook.

The analysis of Nestlé's sales and revenues is crucial for understanding the financial performance and overall health of the company. However, it's important to consider various factors that can impact these metrics.

One significant event affecting Nestlé's sales was the sale of part of its stake in the cosmetics business L'Oréal in 2014. This transaction likely led to a decline in sales figures for that period, as it involved divesting a portion of the company's assets. Such strategic decisions can have both short-term and long-term implications for a company's financial performance, including its sales and revenue streams.

Additionally, Nestlé, like other companies in the food and beverage sector, is operating in a challenging environment characterized by several factors. One of these challenges is the pressure on profit margins. Companies may find it difficult to raise prices for their products due to various reasons, including intense competition and consumer price sensitivity. This can constrain revenue growth and impact overall sales figures.

Furthermore, productivity challenges add another layer of complexity to the situation. If companies are experiencing a decline in productivity, it can affect their ability to efficiently produce goods and services, which may ultimately impact sales and revenue generation.

The insights provided by Koen De Leus, a senior economist at KBC in Brussels, highlight the broader economic context in which Nestlé operates. His observation about the challenging environment facing companies in the sector underscores the importance of understanding external factors that can influence sales and revenue performance.

3.4 MAIN COMPETITORS

Nestlé operates in a diverse range of markets within the food and beverage industry, which means it faces competition from various companies with different focuses and specialties. To analyze its competitive landscape, we've identified five key competitors based on ratings and reports: Danone, Mondelez, Unilever, Mars, and Pladis.

Danone is known for producing and selling healthy and delicious food tailored to the needs of consumers of all ages. Mondelez offers a variety of products including chocolate, cookies, and confectionery. Unilever is a major producer of consumer goods, including food and beverage products, with an extensive distribution network. Mars is renowned for its confectionery products and holds a leading position in the industry. Pladis Ltd specializes in biscuits, chocolate, and confectionery on a global scale.

While these companies compete with Nestlé across various markets, it's important to note that Nestlé also faces competition from specialized companies in each specific market it operates in. For example, in the coffee market, Nestlé competes with companies like Starbucks, Keurig, and Maxwell House, which are known for their expertise and focus in this particular segment.

3.5. MARKET SHARE

Nestlé boasts a diverse business portfolio that spans various product categories such as water, coffee, health products, and chocolate, among others. While Nestlé operates across multiple segments, a significant portion of its sales is attributed to chocolate products. Therefore, for our analysis, we will primarily focus on the global chocolate market to assess Nestlé's performance and market share trends. However, it's crucial to consider Nestlé as a whole to gain a comprehensive understanding of its strengths and weaknesses.

Examining the global chocolate market, we can observe Nestlé's market share from 2012 to 2016, as depicted in Figure 6. Despite Nestlé's substantial presence in the market, the data reveals a declining trend in its market share over the years. While Nestlé still commands a significant portion of the market, this downward trajectory could be a cause for concern for investors and analysts.

A declining market share may indicate challenges or weaknesses within Nestlé's chocolate segment, such as increased competition, shifting consumer preferences, or operational inefficiencies. As such, it is imperative for Nestlé to address these issues and implement strategies to reverse this trend and enhance its competitiveness in the global chocolate market.

Investors and stakeholders closely monitor market share trends as they provide insights into a company's performance, market positioning, and growth prospects. Therefore, it is essential for Nestlé to take proactive measures to stabilize or increase its market share in the chocolate segment, ensuring sustained growth and profitability in the long run.

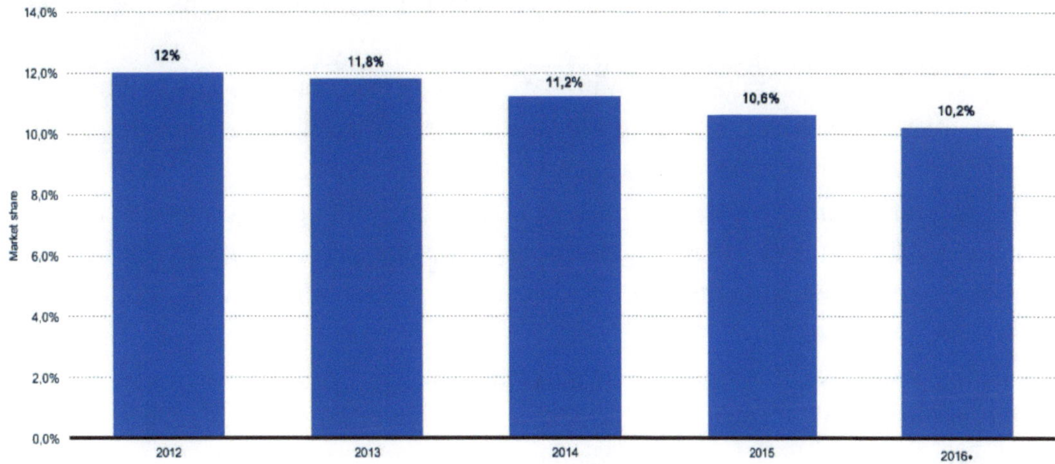

Figure 6. Market share of Nestlé on Global Chocolate market.
Source: Statista. Wall Street Journal.

Strengths: Nestlé, the largest food company globally, boasts an impressive array of strengths that underpin its market dominance and enduring success. Let's frame these strengths more succinctly:

1. Market Capitalization and Stability: With a market cap exceeding $307.4 billion, Nestlé's high valuation attracts investors, providing access to capital without relying heavily on loans. This stability is crucial for long-term growth and public confidence.
2. Respected Brand Name: Nestlé has invested heavily in building strong brand equity, focusing on customer satisfaction, and fostering genuine relationships. Through smart marketing, it has associated its brand with qualities like purity, nutrition, and family bonds, epitomized by its slogan "Good food, Good life."
3. High Brand Value: Nestlé's brand value, estimated at $20.8 billion, reflects its solid financial position, robust supply chain, global presence, and diverse portfolio of successful sub-brands. This high brand value attracts investors and enhances customer confidence.
4. Diversified Brand Portfolio: With over 2000 sub-brands, including household names like Nescafé, KitKat, and Purina, Nestlé enjoys stability and profitability across various sectors within the food industry, mitigating risks through diversification.
5. Global Presence: Operating in over 186 countries, Nestlé dominates markets worldwide, with significant sales shares across the Americas, Europe, Africa, and Asia. This extensive reach ensures market leadership and revenue diversification.
6. Environmental Sustainability: Nestlé prioritizes environmental sustainability, reducing greenhouse gas emissions, committing to carbon neutrality, and adopting eco-friendly practices. This aligns with growing consumer demand for environmentally responsible brands.
7. Focus on Healthy Food Options: Nestlé not only offers tasty food but also prioritizes nutritional value, reducing sugar content and fortifying products for improved health. This enhances its brand image and addresses consumer concerns about wellness.
8. Strategic Partnerships and Acquisitions: Nestlé leverages partnerships and acquisitions to expand its global reach, enhance competitiveness, and access new markets and technologies. Key partnerships with brands like Starbucks and acquisitions bolster its position in the industry.
9. Efficient Research and Development: With the largest R&D department in the food and beverage industry, Nestlé invests in innovation to enhance product quality, safety, and nutritional content, driving customer satisfaction and market differentiation.
10. Efficient Distribution System: Despite promoting local supply chains, Nestlé maintains a highly efficient global distribution network, ensuring the timely delivery of products and raw materials worldwide. This logistical prowess supports its global operations and market leadership.

Weaknesses: Despite its formidable position in the market, Nestlé faces challenges that can impact its operations and reputation. Here's a more concise framing of these challenges:

1. Inflationary Pressure and Price Hikes: Inflationary pressures, exacerbated by factors like the Ukraine conflict, increase Nestlé's production costs, squeezing profit margins. This forces the

company to implement price hikes, potentially affecting customer demand and affordability, especially in low-income regions.

2. Fluctuations in Cocoa prices : The rise in cocoa prices in 2023/24 poses a threat to Nestlé due to its significant impact on the global chocolate market. As one of the world's leading producers of chocolate products, Nestlé heavily relies on cocoa as a key ingredient. When cocoa prices increase, it directly affects the cost of production for Nestlé, potentially leading to decreased profit margins or the need to raise prices for consumers. Additionally, if Nestlé chooses not to pass on the increased costs to consumers by raising prices, it could impact their competitiveness within the chocolate market, as consumers may opt for cheaper alternatives from competitors. This could result in a loss of market share for Nestlé.Furthermore, fluctuations in cocoa prices can also disrupt the supply chain and procurement processes for Nestlé, leading to potential challenges in sourcing quality cocoa at affordable prices. This could further impact production efficiency and overall profitability for the company.

3. Complex Organizational Structure: Nestlé's expansive global presence necessitates a complex organizational structure to manage diverse supply chains and customer segments worldwide. However, this complexity comes with significant financial and manpower costs, as well as the risk of redundancy and slow decision-making.

4. Controversies and Backlash: Nestlé has faced a range of controversies globally, including accusations of depriving indigenous communities of water resources, food safety issues with products like Maggi noodles in India, and allegations of child labor in its cocoa supply chain. These controversies have damaged the company's reputation and led to legal and financial repercussions.

5. Expensive Advertising Model: Despite its size, Nestlé relies heavily on traditional advertising channels, resulting in high customer acquisition costs. Its advertising expenses, totaling $9.2 billion in 2020, strain its financial resources.

6. Allegations of Poor Product Quality: Nestlé's reputation for product quality is tarnished by allegations of contamination and poor quality control, particularly given its vast portfolio of brands operating across different regions. These incidents expose the company to litigation and consumer distrust.

Opportunities:

1. Collaborating with Startups: Nestlé partners with innovative startups through programs like the Nestlé Innovation Accelerator, investing in companies like Blue Bottle Coffee and Freshly to drive growth and stay ahead in the market.

2. Expanding Online Presence: Nestlé is expanding its e-commerce capabilities through partnerships with major platforms like Amazon and Alibaba, as well as launching its own global e-commerce platform, the Nestlé Virtual Store.

3. Expanding into Key Sectors: Nestlé expands its presence in trending sectors like coffee, bottled water, and pet food through strategic acquisitions and investments, while also making inroads into new markets like vegan food and China.

4. Improving Reputation: Nestlé focuses on transparency, sustainability, and corporate social responsibility to address negative perceptions and improve its reputation, with initiatives like supporting community programs and implementing stricter supply chain policies.

5. Streamlining Organizational Structure: Nestlé streamlines its operations by restructuring into three zones, implementing shared services, and introducing global platforms, reducing costs and improving efficiency.
6. Focusing on Profitable Ventures: Nestlé conducts market research to identify profitable opportunities and evaluates existing ventures to allocate resources effectively and focus on high-profit ventures.

Threats:

1. Inflationary Pressure and Price Hikes: Inflationary pressures increase production costs, leading to price hikes that may impact customer demand and affordability, especially in low-income regions.
2. Complex Organizational Structure: Nestlé's complex structure incurs high costs and risks redundancy and slow decision-making.
3. Controversies and Backlash: Nestlé faces backlash from controversies like water depletion, food safety issues, and allegations of child labor, impacting its reputation and leading to legal and financial repercussions.
4. Expensive Advertising Model: Nestlé's heavy reliance on traditional advertising channels strains financial resources, posing challenges in cost-effective customer acquisition.
5. Allegations of Poor Product Quality: Nestlé's reputation for product quality is undermined by incidents of contamination and poor quality control, risking consumer distrust and litigation.
6. Changes in Consumer Sentiment: Evolving consumer preferences towards healthier, eco-friendly, and convenient packaged goods challenge Nestlé to adapt its product offerings and marketing strategies to meet changing demands.

Political Factors:

Political factors indeed play a significant role in shaping the operational landscape for multinational corporations like Nestlé, which operates across numerous countries. These factors encompass a wide range of policies and regulations related to import, export, taxation, labor laws, environmental standards, and more. Keeping abreast of these changes is crucial for Nestlé to navigate potential challenges and capitalize on opportunities in different markets.

For instance, stringent labor laws, especially those aimed at eradicating child labor in cocoa farms, can directly impact Nestlé's cocoa supply chain and production processes. Such regulations may necessitate adjustments to sourcing practices and operational protocols, potentially leading to increased costs or disruptions in supply.

The uncertainty surrounding events like Brexit can also pose significant challenges for companies like Nestlé, as it introduces volatility and instability in the business environment. The prospect of regulatory changes, trade barriers, and economic uncertainties can prompt strategic reassessment of operations, including considerations of relocation to mitigate risks.

Moreover, changes in food regulations, such as those experienced with Nestlé's Maggi product, require meticulous scrutiny and adaptation to ensure compliance while meeting consumer expectations. This entails extensive testing and innovation to reformulate products without compromising on quality or taste, which can be both resource-intensive and time-consuming.

However, not all political developments pose challenges for Nestlé. Favorable policies, such as corporate tax reductions, as witnessed in India's latest budget, can provide opportunities for cost savings and increased competitiveness. Lower tax burdens enable Nestlé to invest more in research, development, and production, ultimately leading to enhanced product quality and affordability for consumers.

In essence, the ability of Nestlé to navigate through the complexities of political factors hinges on its agility, adaptability, and strategic foresight. By closely monitoring regulatory changes, engaging with stakeholders, and proactively addressing challenges, Nestlé can mitigate risks and capitalize on opportunities to drive sustainable growth and societal impact.

Economic Factors:

Operating in multiple countries exposes Nestlé to a diverse array of economic conditions, necessitating the formulation of various economic policies tailored to each market. One of the primary objectives of these policies is to ensure affordability while delivering quality food products to consumers, amidst the backdrop of fluctuating raw material prices influenced by political and environmental factors.

The escalation of trade tensions between major economies like China and the US has led to increased volatility in raw material prices, posing challenges for Nestlé's supply chain management. This, coupled with stagnant disposable incomes in some regions, has made it challenging to maintain product affordability without compromising on quality.

Moreover, deflationary pressures, as observed in Western Europe, further exacerbate pricing challenges for Nestlé. Economic factors such as fluctuations in exchange rates or political unrest can contribute to such deflationary trends, impacting consumer purchasing power and overall market demand.

In response to these challenges, Nestlé has implemented initiatives to promote local-level production of raw materials, thereby enhancing the efficiency and resilience of agricultural sectors across its operating countries. By reducing reliance on imported materials and fostering local sourcing, Nestlé can mitigate risks associated with external market fluctuations and enhance supply chain stability.

Furthermore, given that the US and China are key markets for Nestlé, improvements in economic activity in these regions are pivotal for driving overall performance, sales growth, and profitability. Economic stability and growth in these markets translate into increased consumer spending power, leading to higher demand for Nestlé products and improved financial outcomes for the company.

Social Factors:

Nestlé operates within a constantly evolving consumer landscape characterized by shifting preferences, demographics, and cultural nuances. As consumer tastes continue to change, Nestlé must proactively adapt to meet the demand for health-conscious, organic, and plant-based products. Demographic changes, such as aging populations and increasing income levels, also influence consumer preferences, particularly towards health and wellness offerings. Nestlé's success hinges on its ability to understand and respond to these trends effectively.

Moreover, cultural considerations are essential as Nestlé operates across diverse markets globally. To succeed, Nestlé must grasp local customs and tastes, tailoring its product development and marketing strategies accordingly. Additionally, ethical considerations like sustainability and fair trade play a significant role in shaping brand perception and consumer loyalty. Nestlé is responding to these demands by developing healthier product ranges and implementing sustainable practices throughout its value chain.

In response to growing consumer awareness, Nestlé is prioritizing product quality and safety measures to mitigate health risks across its operations. Anticipating customer needs and offering innovative, high-quality products remain central to Nestlé's strategy for maintaining competitiveness and relevance in the market.

Furthermore, Nestlé is investing in sustainable initiatives, such as the construction of solar plants, to align with consumer preferences for environmentally friendly practices. Addressing concerns about canned and precooked foods, Nestlé is actively engaged in research and development to provide scientific evidence and dispel misconceptions.

To meet evolving customer demands, Nestlé is also introducing customized products like the Nestle KitKat in the UK market, demonstrating its commitment to innovation and customer satisfaction. Overall, Nestlé's multifaceted approach to navigating market dynamics underscores its dedication to sustainability, innovation, and meeting the needs of diverse consumer segments for long-term success.

Technological Factors:

Nestlé is committed to integrating digital solutions, services, and models both internally and externally, recognizing the transformative potential of technology. However, as cyber-attacks pose a significant threat to data reliability, security, and privacy, Nestlé acknowledges the importance of developing contingency plans to mitigate risks associated with digital expansion.

To enhance operational efficiency and sustainability, Nestlé is investing in start-ups to leverage real-time data for water quality monitoring, enabling more efficient water consumption. Additionally, Nestlé is exploring the use of blockchain technology to improve transparency within its supply chain, demonstrating its willingness to embrace innovative solutions to drive change.

Furthermore, Nestlé is actively engaging with consumers by providing access to nutritional information through various digital platforms. For instance, Nestlé has partnered with governments to develop portals for consumers to access detailed information about its products' nutrition content. In the United States, Nestlé participates in the SmartLabel® transparency initiative, offering online access to nutrition, ingredient, and allergen information for a significant portion of its product portfolio.

Legal Factors:

Nestlé's commitment to creating shared value and achieving zero environmental impact through its operations underscores its dedication to environmental sustainability. One of the company's key initiatives is reducing the use of plastic in its products and transitioning to 100% recyclable plastic in all its packaging materials. Given that Nestlé is among the major contributors to global plastic production, these efforts represent a significant stride towards mitigating environmental harm.

As countries worldwide prioritize sustainability, Nestlé must closely monitor and adapt to evolving environmental policies across its diverse operational regions. Failure to comply with regulations, such as the palm oil sustainability reporting requirement that led to Nestlé's suspension by the RSPO, can result in significant setbacks for the company.

Nestlé's sustainability efforts extend beyond reducing plastic usage. The company has reported a 2.6% reduction in indirect greenhouse gas emissions per tonne of product produced and boasts 293 companies under its umbrella claiming zero-waste production. Moreover, Nestlé is actively developing plant-based offerings and promoting sustainable nutrition practices globally.

Water efficiency and sustainability are also focal points of Nestlé's sustainability agenda, with initiatives aimed at promoting responsible water usage across its operations and advocating for water stewardship.

Nestlé's origins trace back to the mid-1860s in Switzerland when Henri Nestlé devised one of the earliest baby formulas. Henri recognized the urgent need for a nutritious and affordable alternative for mothers unable to breastfeed, a necessity underscored by the tragic toll of infant malnutrition at the time. His groundbreaking concoction, named Farine Lactée, proved lifesaving for an ailing premature baby, marking the dawn of Nestlé's legacy in nourishment innovation.

As Nestlé flourished, it encountered pivotal moments that shaped its trajectory. In 1874, under the stewardship of Jules Monnerat, Nestlé crafted its condensed milk, sparking competition with the Anglo-Swiss Condensed Milk Company. This rivalry culminated in a merger in 1905, fortifying Nestlé's foothold in Europe and beyond. Despite the adversities of World War I, Nestlé's strategic expansion into the United States buoyed its resilience, though post-war challenges tested its mettle.

Undeterred, Nestlé embarked on a path of diversification and globalization. The interwar period heralded iconic creations like Nescafé, revolutionizing coffee consumption, and Nestea, broadening its beverage portfolio. World War II posed fresh hurdles, but Nestlé's adaptability saw it thrive, particularly with the surge in demand fueled by American servicemen.

The post-war era witnessed Nestlé's ascent as a global powerhouse through strategic acquisitions spanning diverse sectors. From culinary delights like Crosse & Blackwell to frozen favorites like Stouffer's, Nestlé's portfolio burgeoned. Amid economic turbulence and social scrutiny, Nestlé navigated controversies, notably the boycott over its marketing practices in developing countries, striving to align with global health standards.

Embracing innovation, Nestlé ventured into pharmaceuticals and cosmetics, diversifying its offerings. Collaborations with industry giants like L'Oréal underscored Nestlé's vision for sustained growth. Despite periodic challenges, Nestlé's steadfast commitment to quality and adaptability propelled it through successive decades, culminating in landmark acquisitions like Carnation and Ralston Purina.

Today, Nestlé stands as a titan in the global food industry, with a sprawling network of factories and an unwavering dedication to long-term prosperity. With a keen eye on innovation and sustainability, Nestlé continues to shape the culinary landscape, poised to usher in a new era of culinary excellence and social responsibility.

Nestle's matrix organizational structure is a sophisticated framework that blends the strengths of both functional and divisional structures. This approach allows Nestle to effectively manage its diverse portfolio of products and geographic markets while maintaining a cohesive organizational identity.

At the core of Nestle's structure are its various business segments, each responsible for specific product categories or geographic regions. These segments, such as Nestlé Waters, Nestle Nutrition, and Nestlé Health Science, operate with a considerable degree of autonomy. This autonomy enables them to tailor their strategies and operations to meet the unique demands and opportunities within their respective markets.

The global scope of Nestle's operations is reflected in its organizational structure, with a vast network of subsidiaries and branches spanning over 186 countries. This global presence necessitates a structure that can accommodate the complexities of operating in diverse cultural, economic, and regulatory environments.

Within the matrix structure, Nestle maintains several functional departments, including marketing, finance, research and development, and human resources. These departments provide essential support to the business segments, ensuring the efficient functioning of the company as a whole. For example, the marketing department helps develop and implement marketing strategies tailored to different markets, while the research and development department drives innovation and product development efforts.

Nestle's history of decentralization further enhances its ability to adapt to local market conditions and consumer preferences. By granting individual business units a significant degree of independence and control over their operations, Nestle can respond swiftly to changes in the competitive landscape or shifts in consumer behavior.

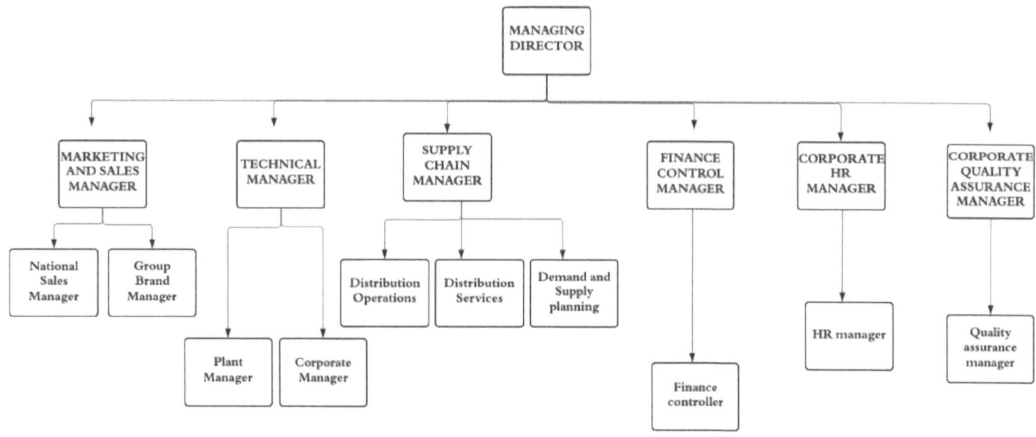

The company's commitment to global business excellence is evident in its ongoing efforts to drive efficiency, effectiveness, and continuous improvement throughout the organization. These initiatives often involve sharing best practices and leveraging synergies across different business units to optimize performance and enhance competitiveness.

Nestle also prioritizes corporate social responsibility (CSR) within its organizational structure. The company has dedicated departments and teams focused on sustainability and responsible business practices, integrating these principles into its overall strategy and operations.

Ultimately, Nestle's organizational structure is shaped by its top leadership, including the CEO and executive team. Their decisions and strategic direction influence how the company is organized and operated, ensuring alignment with overarching business goals and objectives. Through its matrix structure and emphasis on autonomy, collaboration, and CSR, Nestle is well-positioned to navigate the complexities of the global marketplace while driving sustainable growth and value creation.

Nestlé is grappling with several strategic challenges stemming from its extensive global operations. The company is encountering difficulties managing substantial logistics expenses and storage constraints associated with transporting ingredients and products across borders (Bradley, 2014). Moreover, the effectiveness of coordination and decision-making between country-specific headquarters and sites is gradually diminishing due to Nestlé's expansive international presence and diverse product portfolio. Additionally, the consistent promotion of new and innovative products by Nestlé does not always yield desired results, as certain products or innovations may not resonate with or be suitable for specific regions or countries.

Strategic plan and Action recommendation

<u>Basic strategic direction</u>

Nestlé's strategic mission is to emerge as the global leader in health, nutrition, and wellness. The company's mission statement, "good food and good life," emphasizes its commitment to offering consumers a wide array of nutritious choices across various food and beverage categories. Nestlé pursues four primary strategic objectives: enhancing customers' lives with top-quality products, achieving operational excellence through its dedicated research and development network and talented workforce, continuously innovating to introduce new product lines, and driving financial growth through efficient performance and customer acquisition. Over a five-year period, Nestlé has increased its shareholder returns by 25%.

In terms of overall business strategy, Nestlé has the option to adopt three approaches to maintain a competitive edge in the industry: cost leadership, differentiation, and focus. Upon analyzing Nestlé's business principles, it becomes apparent that the company has opted for a combination of low-cost and product differentiation strategies to outperform its rivals.

Nestlé's differentiation strategy revolves around offering an extensive range of high-quality products at premium price points. Leveraging its robust research and development network, Nestlé has established itself as a leading producer of food and beverages worldwide. This enables Nestlé to deliver innovative and nutritious products that set it apart from competitors. Additionally, Nestlé distinguishes its products through its skilled workforce, unique product features, advanced technology, exceptional services, and impactful advertising campaigns.

<u>Cost-Leadership strategy</u>

Nestlé has effectively employed a cost-leadership strategy to gain a competitive edge. The company focuses on producing and promoting its products at lower costs compared to competitors. This strategy has been facilitated by Nestlé's economies of scale in manufacturing, sourcing raw materials, and marketing. By offering a wide range of products at affordable prices, Nestlé has successfully captured market share and cultivated customer loyalty, particularly in developing countries.

<u>Economic analysis</u>

In 2014, Nestlé achieved remarkable performance, leading to satisfactory dividends for its shareholders. The company's disciplined approach and commitment to driving performance in alignment with its model of resource efficiency and profitable growth were key factors contributing to its success. However, despite this strong performance, Nestlé faced challenges in subsequent years, particularly in generating higher income due to a decline in product sales. As a result, Nestlé needs to refocus its efforts on enhancing its market capabilities and seizing opportunities to expand its organizational activities globally.

The decline in product sales indicates shifting consumer preferences, evolving market dynamics, or intensified competition, among other factors. To address this challenge, Nestlé must reassess its market positioning, product offerings, and marketing strategies to regain momentum and drive growth. This may involve innovating new products, revitalizing existing ones, or exploring new market segments to tap into untapped opportunities.

Furthermore, Nestlé's global expansion strategy plays a crucial role in sustaining long-term growth and profitability. By leveraging its extensive resources, capabilities, and brand presence, Nestlé can explore new markets and regions where demand for its products is high or where there is potential for growth. This may involve investing in infrastructure, distribution networks, and marketing initiatives to strengthen its presence and capture market share in diverse geographic locations.

Figure 1: Net Income of Nestle

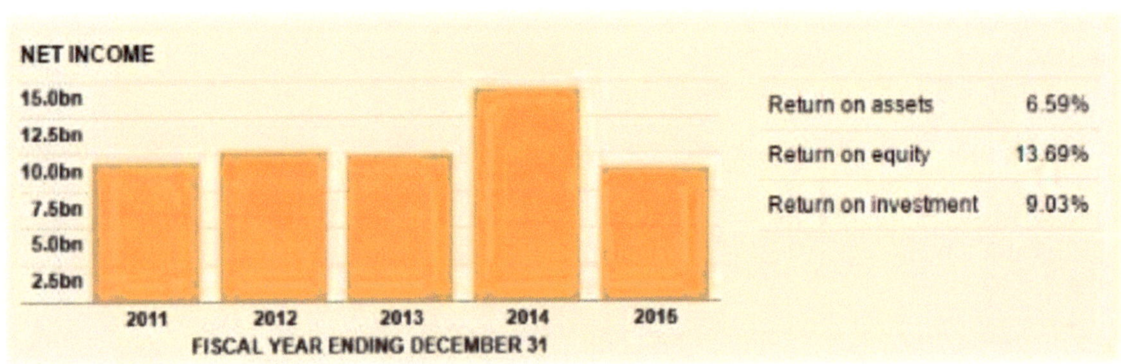

Source: (Financial Times, 2016)

The decline in net income for a company, as seen in Nestlé's case in 2015, can have significant implications for its financial performance metrics, such as return on assets (ROA), return on equity (ROE), and return on investment (ROI). In Nestlé's case, with a decline in net income, the ROA, ROE, and ROI were affected, with ROA at 6.59%, ROE at 13.69%, and ROI at 9.03%. These figures indicate a decrease in the company's profitability and efficiency in utilizing its assets, equity, and investments to generate returns.

A lower ROA suggests that Nestlé's assets are generating less income compared to previous periods, indicating reduced efficiency in asset utilization. Similarly, a lower ROE indicates a decline in the company's ability to generate profits from its shareholders' equity, which can be concerning for investors as it reflects decreased profitability and potential challenges in generating returns on their investment.

Moreover, a lower ROI signifies a decrease in the company's ability to generate returns on its investments, indicating potential inefficiencies or underperformance in utilizing capital to generate profits. This can be problematic for Nestlé as it may struggle to attract and retain investors, maintain market share, and sustain long-term growth and profitability.

Figure 2: Assets and Debt amount of Nestle

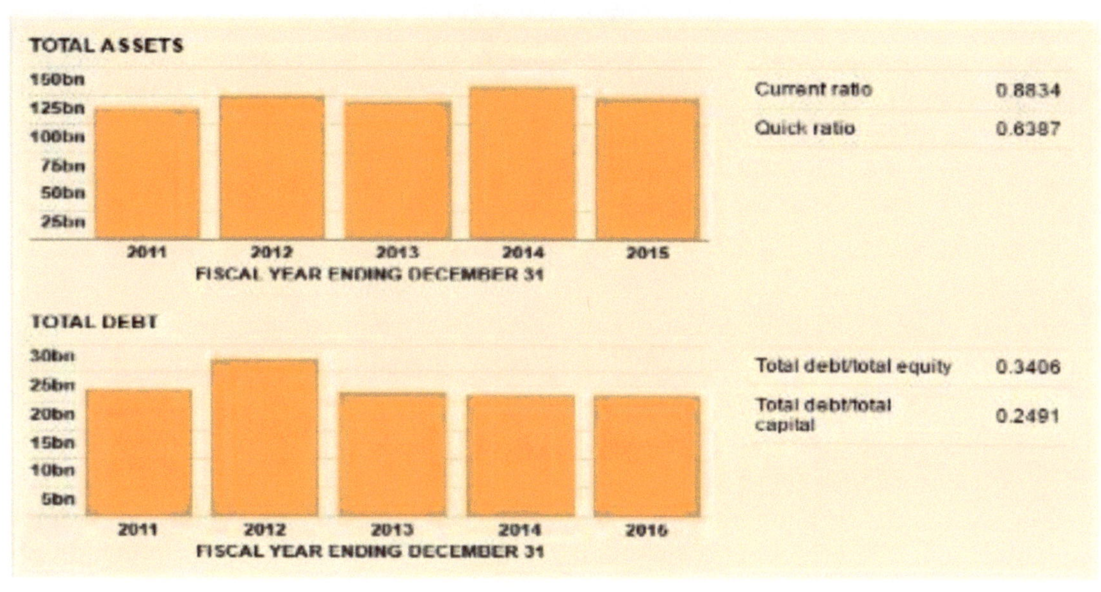

Source: (Financial Times, 2016)

Analyzing the balance sheet of a company can provide valuable insights into its financial health and stability. In the case of Nestlé, if there is inconsistency or fluctuations in the growth of total assets over time, it may suggest varying levels of investment or divestment in the company's assets. This could be due to factors such as acquisitions, disposals, or changes in investment strategies.

However, despite fluctuations in asset growth, the total value of assets exceeds the value of debt. This indicates that Nestlé possesses more assets than liabilities, which can be interpreted as a positive sign of financial strength and stability. With assets exceeding debt, Nestlé has the capacity to leverage its assets to clear its outstanding debt obligations if necessary.

Using assets to clear debt, often referred to as asset-backed financing, can be advantageous for companies like Nestlé with substantial asset bases. By utilizing assets as collateral, Nestlé can secure favorable terms for borrowing or refinance existing debt at lower interest rates. This strategy can help reduce financial risk, lower interest expenses, and improve overall liquidity and solvency.

Furthermore, having a higher value of assets than debt enhances Nestlé's creditworthiness and provides flexibility in managing its capital structure. It offers reassurance to investors, creditors, and stakeholders about the company's ability to meet its financial obligations and sustain operations even during challenging economic conditions.

<u>Ratio and Liquidity Analysis</u>

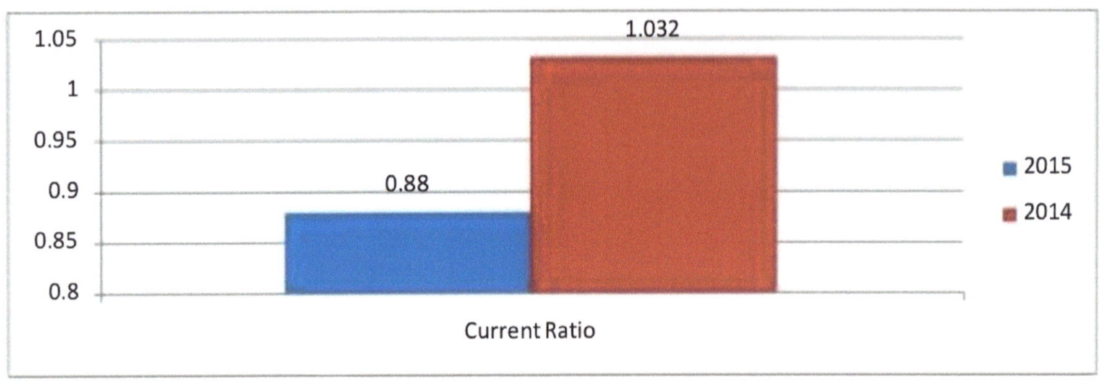

Source: (Nestle, 2016)

When assessing a company's liquidity position, factors such as current assets, current liabilities, and the working capital cycle are crucial indicators. In Nestlé's case, if the liquidity position is deemed unfavorable, it suggests that the company may encounter challenges in managing its working capital effectively.

A liquidity ratio, such as the current ratio or quick ratio, measures a company's ability to meet its short-term obligations using its current assets. If these ratios indicate a lower liquidity position, it implies that Nestlé may have difficulty in covering its short-term liabilities with its current assets.

Furthermore, if Nestlé is taking an extended period to meet its short-term obligations, it could signal inefficiencies in managing its working capital cycle. The working capital cycle encompasses the time it takes for a company to convert its inventory into cash, pay off its liabilities, and receive payments from its customers. If Nestlé's working capital cycle is prolonged, it may lead to cash flow constraints and difficulties in managing day-to-day operations.

Several factors could contribute to Nestlé's liquidity challenges and prolonged working capital cycle. These may include inefficient inventory management, slow receivables collection, or aggressive expansion strategies leading to increased short-term debt obligations.

Addressing these liquidity concerns requires Nestlé to implement effective cash management strategies, improve inventory turnover, streamline receivables collection processes, and optimize its working capital cycle. By enhancing liquidity management practices, Nestlé can strengthen its financial position, ensure timely payment of obligations, and sustain operational efficiency in the long run.

Source: (Nestle, 2016)

The analysis of the graph indicates a concerning trend for the company, particularly in terms of its profit margin, sales performance, and earnings per share (EPS). The declining trend in profit margin over successive years suggests that the company's ability to generate profits from its sales is diminishing. This could be attributed to various factors such as increasing costs, pricing pressures, or declining sales volumes.

Furthermore, the significant drop in sales despite increasing marketing and administration expenses in 2015 is alarming. This discrepancy suggests that the company's investments in marketing and administrative activities may not be yielding the desired results in terms of driving sales growth or market share expansion. This could indicate inefficiencies in resource allocation or ineffective marketing strategies.

The impact of declining sales and profit margins on earnings per share (EPS) is evident, with a notable decrease from 4.54 million in 2014 to 2.90 million in 2015. A decrease in EPS indicates that the company's profitability per share is decreasing, which could adversely affect investor confidence and shareholder returns.

If this performance trend persists in the future, the company could face significant challenges, including potential losses or increased debt levels. A continued decline in sales and profitability could strain the company's financial resources, hinder its ability to meet financial obligations, and erode shareholder value.

To address these challenges and mitigate the risk of further financial deterioration, the company may need to reassess its business strategies, streamline operations, optimize cost structures, and implement effective sales and marketing initiatives to stimulate revenue growth and improve profitability. Additionally, proactive measures to enhance operational efficiency and financial performance are essential to safeguard the company's long-term sustainability and competitiveness in the market.

Source: (Nestle, 2016)

The analysis of the graph suggests that Nestlé has increasingly relied on debt rather than equity to finance its projects or operations, as indicated by the rising debt-to-equity ratio, particularly in 2015. This trend implies that the company has been borrowing more funds relative to its equity capital, potentially to support growth initiatives, capital expenditures, or other financial commitments.

While debt can be an effective means of financing expansion or investment opportunities, excessive reliance on debt can also pose significant financial risks. A high debt-to-equity ratio may signal increased leverage, making the company more vulnerable to fluctuations in interest rates, economic downturns, or unexpected financial challenges. Additionally, higher debt levels can lead to higher interest expenses, reducing profitability and cash flow available for other purposes.

Moreover, if Nestlé is unable to generate sufficient cash flow to meet its debt obligations, it could face liquidity issues and potentially default on its debt payments. This scenario could negatively impact the company's credit rating, increase borrowing costs, and erode investor confidence, leading to further financial instability and potential downward pressure on the company's stock price.

To mitigate these risks, Nestlé may need to take proactive measures to manage its debt levels effectively. This could involve implementing strategies to reduce debt, such as refinancing existing debt at lower interest rates, improving operational efficiency to generate higher cash flows, or divesting non-core assets to reduce financial strain. Additionally, the company may need to reassess its capital structure and consider raising additional equity capital to strengthen its financial position and reduce reliance on debt financing.

Financial Forecast

The market performance and opportunities of Nestlé's brand play a significant role in forecasting potential changes in dividends for subsequent fiscal years. A company's dividend policy is often influenced by its financial performance, cash flow generation, growth prospects, and shareholder expectations.

In the case of Nestlé, if the brand's market performance is strong and opportunities for growth are promising, it can indicate positive prospects for future earnings and cash flow. This, in turn, may enable the company to increase its dividend payments to shareholders. Factors such as increasing sales, expanding market share, successful product launches, and effective cost management can contribute to improved financial performance and enhanced ability to distribute dividends.

On the other hand, if market conditions are challenging, or if Nestlé faces obstacles such as declining sales, increased competition, or economic uncertainties, it may exert downward pressure on dividend growth. In such scenarios, the company may prioritize preserving cash reserves or allocating funds towards strategic initiatives aimed at revitalizing business performance.

In forecasting a 2.27% increase in dividends, Nestlé likely considers various factors, including its historical dividend payout ratios, earnings growth projections, cash flow generation capacity, and long-term financial objectives. By analyzing these metrics alongside market trends and opportunities, Nestlé can make informed decisions about dividend policy adjustments that align with shareholder interests while ensuring sustainable business growth and financial stability.

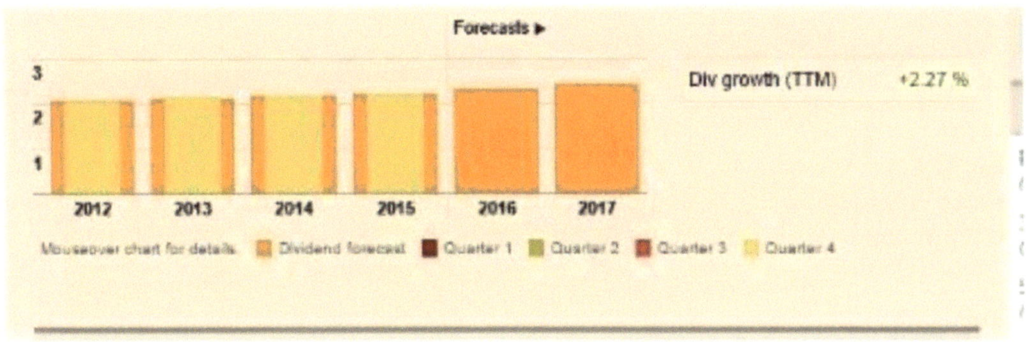

Source: (Markets.ft, 2016)

Figure 7: Revenue Growth Forecast

Source: (Markets.ft, 2016)

Despite experiencing declines in sales revenue and profit, it is anticipated that the company will achieve a 1.63% annual increase in revenue. This growth is expected to be driven by investments in product quality and marketing initiatives, which are poised to generate positive revenue outcomes in the future.

Nestlé's strategic trajectory

Nestlé's international market strategy has been pivotal in driving its growth and establishing a strong presence in consumer products worldwide. With a substantial portion of its revenue, approximately 95%, originating from international markets, Nestlé's global geographic organizational structure has facilitated its proactive involvement in expanding its international business operations rapidly (Markides and Charitou, 2004). Leveraging stable technology and mature product lines, Nestlé aims to achieve low-cost manufacturing in various international countries, enhancing its competitiveness and market reach.

To capitalize on new market opportunities, Nestlé has pursued strategic mergers and acquisitions. For instance, by merging with the manufacturer of Maggi soups and seasonings and acquiring Crosse and Blackwell, a renowned British manufacturer of canned and preserved foods, Nestlé has diversified its product portfolio and strengthened its market position (Mohajan, 2015). These acquisitions align with Nestlé's objective of expanding its presence in the food industry while leveraging its existing expertise and resources.

Furthermore, Nestlé has forged strategic alliances and joint ventures to broaden its business scope and explore new growth areas. Collaborating with Coca-Cola and Beverage Partner Worldwide in joint ventures, Nestlé has shifted its focus from milk and confectionery items to beverages, particularly black tea and green tea (Mohajan, 2015). Such alliances enable Nestlé to capitalize on emerging market trends and consumer preferences while leveraging its brand image as a key competitive advantage.

In addition to expanding its core businesses, Nestlé has ventured into new segments such as fitness and nutricosmetics through joint ventures with industry leaders like L'oreal. For example, the establishment of Inneov, a nutricosmetics brand, demonstrates Nestlé's commitment to innovation and diversification (Nestlé, 2011). By leveraging its research and development capabilities, Nestlé continues to lead the industry in innovation, ensuring maximum flexibility in its product portfolio to meet evolving consumer needs and preferences.

Nestle's extensive portfolio of products caters to a diverse range of consumers across the globe. The brand's target audience can be divided into several segments based on demographic, geographic, and psychographic factors.

Demographically, Nestle's target audience includes individuals of all ages, from infants to seniors. The brand's infant formula products cater to new mothers, while its chocolate and confectionery products appeal to children and young adults. Nestle's range of coffee and tea products targets adults, while its health and wellness products cater to seniors.

Geographically, Nestle has a global presence, with its products available in over 190 countries. The brand's target audience includes individuals from different cultures and backgrounds, and Nestle has adapted its marketing strategies to cater to local preferences and tastes.

Psychographically, Nestle's target audience includes health-conscious individuals who are looking for nutritious and wholesome products that enhance their overall well-being. The brand's focus on health and wellness has made it a popular choice among consumers who are looking to lead a healthier lifestyle.

In addition to the above factors, Nestle's target audience also includes pet owners, as the brand has a range of pet food products. Nestle's target audience is also diverse in terms of income level, with products available at various price points to cater to different budgets. Nestle's target audience includes individuals from all walks of life who are looking for high-quality, nutritious, and delicious products that enhance their overall well-being

For Kids:
Nestle recognizes the importance of providing nutrition and promoting healthy growth among children. Products like Koko Krunch, Caregrow, and Lactogrow are specifically formulated to address the nutritional requirements of growing kids. Koko Krunch offers a delicious breakfast cereal option packed with essential vitamins and minerals, while Caregrow and Lactogrow provide supplementary nutrition to support children's overall development and immune health.

For Working Professionals:
In today's fast-paced world, convenience and freshness are paramount for working professionals who lead busy lives. Nestle's offerings such as Sunrise and Nescafe cater to this segment by providing quick and convenient beverage solutions. Sunrise offers instant breakfast options, including cereal and oats, while Nescafe provides a range of coffee products that are easy to prepare and deliver a refreshing boost of energy to kickstart the day.

For the General Audience:
Nestle's iconic products like Maggi, KitKat, and Milkmaid have achieved widespread popularity among consumers of all ages and backgrounds. Maggi, known for its instant noodles and pasta, offers a convenient and versatile meal solution for busy families. KitKat, with its crispy wafer and creamy

chocolate layers, appeals to consumers seeking a satisfying snack indulgence. Milkmaid, a staple in many households, provides a convenient way to enjoy sweet treats like desserts and beverages.

PRODUCTS

Nestlé's product strategy stands as a core pillar in their successful marketing mix, distinguished by its clear focus on diversity and quality. It is a strategic game plan that propels Nestlé's global recognition and acceptance.

Under this umbrella, the company manages a broad portfolio of thousands of brands, which include renowned global icons like Nescafé, KitKat, Maggi, and Nestea. Furthermore, it takes pride in housing local favorites specific to different countries. This vast array of products caters to the varying tastes, preferences, nutritional needs, and economic capabilities of consumers worldwide. From every-day grocery items to luxury chocolates, health products to pet food – the product range of Nestlé is diverse and widespread.

While quantity and diversity form a significant part of their strategy, quality is one aspect where Nestlé never compromises. Every product launched under the Nestlé banner meets stringent quality standards. Regardless of where it's produced or sold, every product upholds the promise of taste and nutrition that consumers associate with Nestlé.

Innovation is another cornerstone of Nestlé's product strategy. Living in an era where consumers' needs, preferences, and expectations are ever-evolving, staying static is not an option for brands. Understanding this, Nestlé invests heavily in research and development to innovate its products continuously. This continuous innovation spans across improving the nutritional value of products, meeting changing dietary requirements, adapting to new cooking habits, or even launching entirely new products. In essence, innovation at Nestlé is about keeping the product portfolio relevant and desirable to its consumer base.

Moreover, Nestlé pays close attention to packaging designs. A key part of their product strategy, they design packaging not just for aesthetics but also convenience and sustainability. They continually work on minimizing environmental impact and enhancing user experience.

Nestle's marketing strategy focuses on its product portfolio, which includes a wide range of food and beverage items. Some of the most popular categories of Nestle's products are-

<u>Baby Foods</u>

Nestle's marketing strategy includes supplying baby food for babies of all ages through popular brands like Gerber, Nestle Cerelac, and Nestle NaturNes. These brands offer a wide range of easily-digested nutritious instant cereals that are not a substitute for breast milk but can sufficiently meet the nutritional requirements of a growing baby.

- NESTLE CERELAC
- GERBER APPLE STRAWBERRY BANANA

Bottled Waters

Nestle bottled water has spread its product presence to more than 100 countries. Nestle Waters bottles natural mineral waters through brands like Perrier, Acqua Panna, Vittel, Buxton, Erikli, and S. Pellegrino to provide high-quality and sustainable hydration.

- NESTLE'S PURE LIFE
- PERRIER
- ACQUA PANNA NATURAL MINERAL WATER
- BUXTON MINERAL WATER

Dairy Products

Nestle dairy products boast excellent quality milk products that are popular worldwide. The Health and wellness segment relies on milk and dairy products, especially Nido. Nestle ice creams made from milk in different flavors are also top-rated worldwide.

- NESTLE SLIM
- NESTLE MILK

Chilled and Frozen Food

Nestle serves chilled and frozen foods with the help of brands like Thomy, Garden Gourmet, and Digiorno.

- GARDEN GOURMET MINI FILLETS
- THOMY SALAD DRESSINGS

Liquid and Powdered Beverages

Nestle deals in the beverage category with the help of the most popular and prominent coffee brand, Nescafe. Nestle tea, chocolate, and malt beverages are equally popular. It also offers nutritional drinks through brands like Boost that have the right amount of minerals, vitamins, and protein to keep individuals healthy, fit, and refined.

- NESCAFE GOLD BLEND
- BOOST MALT BEVERAGE
- NESTEA ICED TEA

Chocolates

Nestle is active in the chocolate segment through KitKat, Aero, Milky Bar, and Eclairs. The brand has introduced Alpino chocolate as part of its gifting segment marketing strategy to target rival brands, especially Cadbury's products.

- AERO CHOCOLATE BAR
- CAILLER CHOCOLATE
- KITKAT PEANUT BUTTER

Ready-to-Cook Foods

Several Nestle products are in the ready-to-cook category, like instant noodles from Maggi.

- MAGGI SOUPS
- MAGGI SEASONINGS

Breakfast Cereal

Nestle offers breakfast cereals with the help of several brands like Cheerios and Fitness as a balanced diet for every age and healthy lifestyle.

- MULTIGRAIN CHEERIOS FIBRE 5 WHOLE GRAINS
- FITNESS TOASTIES
- NESQUIK BREAKFAST CEREAL

Prepared Dishes and Cooking Aids

The company has also introduced the concept of prepared dishes in local flavors to benefit consumers too busy to prepare food from scratch. Popular Nestle brands like Buitoni, Stouffer's, and Maggi cater to regional tastes with the help of its renowned products.

- DIGIORNO CRISPY PAN PIZZA
- MAGGI 2-MINUTE NOODLES

Pet Care

Nestle's products in the pet category include wholesome kibbles and dry dog food from brands like Bakers Complete and Beneful. Each box contains various varieties and flavors to satisfy your pet's cravings. Nestle offers cat food in multiple formulas with the help of its brands, Cat Chow, Friskies, and Felix.

- BAKERS COMPLETE WITH TASTY BEEF AND COUNTRY VEGETABLES
- BENEFUL ORIGINAL
- PURINA CAT CHOW

PRICING:

Nestle's pricing strategy varies depending on the product category and target market. The brand's premium products, such as gourmet coffee, are priced higher, while its everyday products, such as instant coffee, are priced lower to appeal to budget-conscious consumers. Nestle's pricing strategy is also influenced by local market conditions and competition.

1. **Price Skimming**: Nestle adopts a price skimming strategy for certain products when entering new markets, initially setting higher prices to target upper-middle-class consumers. As products become established, prices are gradually lowered to appeal to broader market segments, such as the middle class.
2. **Inexpensive Pricing Strategy**: Nestle offers fair pricing for a range of its brands, with pricing based on market segmentation. By understanding consumer needs and demographics, Nestle adjusts pricing to appeal to different target audiences.
3. **Bundle Pricing**: Recognizing consumer preferences for bulk purchases, Nestle implements bundle pack offerings to encourage larger purchases and increase sales volume. This strategy has been particularly successful with products like Maggi noodles.
4. **Penetration Pricing**: When introducing new products or flavors, Nestle may initially set lower prices to attract customers away from competitors. Once a customer base is established, prices may be adjusted upwards. This strategy was evident with the launch of new Maggi noodle flavors.
5. **Psychological Pricing**: Nestle leverages psychological pricing techniques, such as setting prices just below round numbers, to create a positive perception among consumers and stimulate purchases. For example, pricing Nestle Aero bliss slightly below a round figure.
6. **Stock Keeping Units (SKU)**: Nestle offers diverse pricing for each stock-keeping unit, catering to different consumer segments. By offering various pack sizes, Nestle ensures its products are accessible to a wider range of consumers.
7. **Discounts**: Nestle provides discounts through various retail channels, often bundling products or offering percentage discounts. This encourages consumers to purchase more and enhances brand loyalty.
8. **Competitive Pricing**: Nestle closely analyzes the pricing strategies of competitors across its brands and adjusts its pricing accordingly. By understanding market dynamics and consumer preferences, Nestle maintains competitiveness in the market.
9. **Global Pricing Strategies**: Internationally, Nestle adapts its pricing strategies to align with regional market conditions and achieve financial objectives. This may involve variations in pricing based on factors like local demand and competition.

Nestle's success stems from its ability to adapt its pricing strategies to diverse markets and consumer segments. By prioritizing consumer needs and offering quality products at different price points, Nestle maximizes sales and profitability across its brand portfolio.

PLACE:

The place strategy forms a crucial facet of Nestlé's overall marketing mix. Also referred to as distribution strategy, it outlines the pathways a product takes from the manufacturer to the end consumer. For Nestlé, an efficient place strategy means ensuring the maximum availability of its products to customers across various locations.

Nestlé's place strategy encompasses both depth and breadth. Depth refers to the company's penetration in a specific market, while breadth implies its reach across multiple geographical locations. To this end, Nestlé has one of the most extensive distribution networks in the world. It operates in over 186 countries and regions with numerous manufacturing facilities strategically placed worldwide. This wide-reaching network allows Nestlé to make its products accessible to consumers wherever they may be.

A key aspect of Nestlé's place strategy is its diversified distribution channels. Nestlé's products are not only available in large supermarkets and hypermarkets but also smaller grocery stores, convenience stores, and online retail platforms. Such diversification ensures that no matter where a customer prefers to shop, they can always find Nestlé's products.

Another component of Nestlé's place strategy is its effective use of direct and indirect distribution methods. In direct distribution, Nestlé supplies products directly to large retail chains or sells directly to consumers through its websites. Indirect distribution involves third-party entities such as wholesalers, distributors, or small retail outlets. This balanced approach helps Nestlé cater to different types of consumers and market segments.

Additionally, Nestlé focuses heavily on optimizing its supply chain management. From procuring raw materials to delivering the finished products to retailers, each step is meticulously planned and executed to ensure efficiency and cost-effectiveness. They continually invest in technologies and practices to improve their supply chain sustainability, aiming for zero environmental impact in their operations.

Nestle has a global presence, with its products available in over 190 countries. The brand's distribution channels include supermarkets, convenience stores, online platforms, and direct-to-consumer channels. Nestle's distribution strategy is aimed at maximizing reach and accessibility to consumers across the globe.

Today, Nestlé Milk Pak manufactures in more than 81 countries and accomplishes 98% of its turnover outside Europe. Nestlé MilkPak is the world's biggest milk organization, which does 98% of its business. It has a yearly turnover of 70 billion Swiss francs, 522 new processing plants in 81 nations, 200 working organizations, 1 fundamental exploration external and 20 mechanical improvement bunches, has more than 231,000 representatives and more than 8000 items around the world.

60% of the buyer's partner quality with Nestle. 57.3 % of the buyers inclines toward Nestle over different brands of immaculate water that are accessible in the business sector .66% shoppers purchased Nestle water due to its image picture which is of good quality items.

PROMOTION:
Nestle's promotion strategy includes advertising, sales promotion, public relations, and personal selling. The brand's advertising campaigns, such as the "Good Food, Good Life" campaign, focus on promoting the health and wellness benefits of its products. Nestle also uses sales promotions, such as discounts and coupons, to incentivize consumers to try its products. The brand's public relations efforts focus on building brand reputation and engaging with consumers through social media and other channels.

Nestle's marketing mix has been instrumental in the brand's success in the highly competitive food and beverage industry. The brand's focus on creating high-quality products that cater to diverse consumer needs, coupled with a well-crafted pricing, distribution, and promotion strategy has helped Nestle maintain its position as a leading player in the market.

Promotion strategy is another vital component of Nestlé's marketing mix. It pertains to the diverse methods and techniques Nestlé employs to communicate with its customers, increase brand awareness, and boost product sales.

Nestlé utilizes an integrated marketing communications approach, where all promotional tools are carefully coordinated to deliver a consistent, clear, and compelling message about the brand and its products. This includes a mix of advertising, sales promotions, public relations, and direct marketing efforts.

Advertising forms a substantial part of Nestlé's promotion strategy. The company invests heavily in television, radio, print media, and digital platforms to reach out to its audience. Their advertisements are designed creatively to capture attention and create a memorable impression. Often, they aim to stir emotions or appeal to the health consciousness of consumers, thus connecting on a deeper level.

Sales promotions are another integral part of Nestlé's promotion strategy. These include temporary incentives like discounts, offers, coupons, contests, or free samples aimed at stimulating quick consumer response. Such tactics are particularly effective during product launches, slow sales periods, or while countering competition.

Nestlé's promotion strategy also prioritizes public relations. The company engages in numerous CSR activities and initiatives focusing on nutrition, water, rural development, sustainability, etc., that resonate well with their corporate mission. They make sure these activities are communicated to the public to foster a positive brand image and build trust among consumers.

Direct marketing is increasingly becoming significant in Nestlé's promotional mix. Through digital marketing initiatives such as emails, social media engagement, SEO optimized content on their websites, or mobile app notifications, Nestlé can reach out to their customers directly and build a more personal relationship.

Last but not least, Nestlé often partners with other brands for co-marketing efforts or sponsors events relevant to its product portfolio. These actions offer additional avenues for brand exposure and customer engagement.

Nestle is a household name, and its marketing campaigns have played a significant role in making it a global brand. Over the years, Nestle has launched numerous successful campaigns, but some have stood out from the rest. Let's take a look at Nestle's most successful campaigns that have captured the hearts of millions.

Nescafe "Open Up" Campaign

The Nescafé "Open Up" campaign stands out as one of Nestlé's most successful marketing endeavors, focusing on fostering human connections over a shared experience of enjoying a cup of coffee. At its core, the campaign aimed to encourage people to connect with one another on a deeper level, transcending barriers and differences through the simple act of sharing stories and experiences over coffee.

The ad featured individuals from diverse backgrounds and walks of life, emphasizing the universal appeal of coffee as a facilitator of conversation and connection. By showcasing authentic interactions and heartfelt moments, the campaign effectively captured the essence of human connection and the role that coffee can play in bringing people together.

One of the key factors contributing to the success of the "Open Up" campaign was its ability to resonate with audiences on an emotional level. The ad tapped into universal themes of friendship, empathy, and shared experiences, striking a chord with viewers and evoking feelings of warmth and nostalgia.

Furthermore, the campaign's message aligns closely with Nescafé's brand identity as a purveyor of moments of connection and togetherness. By positioning coffee as a catalyst for meaningful interactions, Nescafé reinforced its role in people's lives beyond just providing a caffeine boost.

KitKat "Take a Break" Campaign

The KitKat "**Take a Break**" campaign is one of Nestle's most iconic campaigns. The campaign featured the famous "Have a Break, Have a KitKat" tagline. The ad portrayed people taking a break from their busy lives and enjoying a KitKat. The catchy jingle and the memorable tagline made the ad an instant hit.

The enduring success of KitKat's slogan, "Have a break, have a KitKat," lies in its ability to tap into a universal human need for relaxation and indulgence. Since its inception in 1957, this simple yet powerful message has resonated with consumers across generations, transcending cultural boundaries and evolving alongside societal changes.

At its core, the slogan embodies the idea of taking a momentary pause from the hustle and bustle of daily life to savor a small pleasure - in this case, enjoying a KitKat chocolate bar. This concept of self-care and rejuvenation strikes a chord with individuals navigating the stresses of modern living, making KitKat a beloved and trusted brand worldwide.

Throughout its advertising history, KitKat has cleverly leveraged this message to create memorable and impactful commercials that capture the essence of the slogan. The early Elevenses campaign in 1958, for example, targeted British factory workers during their mid-morning tea break, humorously reminding them to "have a break" with a KitKat. This campaign not only reinforced the association between KitKat and relaxation but also ingrained the brand into the cultural fabric of British society.

In subsequent years, KitKat commercials continued to innovate, exploring different scenarios and narratives while staying true to the core message of taking a break. The "No Rest for the Wicked" ad in 1987, featuring a devil and an angel indulging in KitKat during their break, cleverly played on the idea of finding respite even in unexpected situations. This irreverent approach not only entertained audiences but also reinforced KitKat's brand identity as a source of comfort and enjoyment.

The evolution of the slogan in 2001 to "Give Yourself a KitKat. Give Yourself a Break" demonstrated Nestlé's commitment to staying relevant in an ever-changing market landscape. By subtly shifting the focus to self-care and personal well-being, the updated slogan appealed to a new generation of consumers seeking balance in their lives.

In recent years, KitKat has once again adapted its messaging to reflect advancements in technology, particularly the rise of AI. The "Have A(I) Break" campaign cleverly integrates the concept of AI taking breaks to improve accuracy, aligning with KitKat's longstanding message of relaxation and enjoyment. By injecting humor and wit into the narrative, the campaign effectively engages audiences while highlighting the brand's forward-thinking approach.

Overall, the success of KitKat's slogan can be attributed to its timeless appeal and versatility. By tapping into fundamental human desires for relaxation and indulgence, KitKat has created a brand identity that resonates with consumers across generations and continues to thrive in an increasingly competitive market.

Maggi "2-Minute Noodles" Campaign

Maggi's marketing strategies have been instrumental in establishing its iconic status as a convenient and beloved brand in India. Leveraging various advertising channels and communication tactics, Maggi has effectively connected with consumers on both emotional and practical levels.

Iconic ads such as the '2-minute noodles' jingle have ingrained Maggi's convenience proposition into the collective consciousness of Indian consumers. This catchy jingle, coupled with the 'Fast to Cook, Good to Eat' tagline, exemplifies Maggi's commitment to providing quick and tasty meal solutions.

In addition to convenience messaging, Maggi's marketing communications have focused on creating everyday connections and tapping into nostalgia. By embedding Maggi as part of family bonding and associating it with typical Indian dayparts like breakfast and snacktime, the brand has become deeply ingrained in Indian households. Emotional storytelling ads like 'Meri Maggi, Mere Waste' have further strengthened this connection by evoking childhood memories and rituals, driving re-purchase and loyalty among consumers.

Maggi's marketing campaigns have evolved with changing consumer preferences and technological advancements. From celebrity endorsements featuring icons like Madhuri Dixit and Preity Zinta to digital campaigns targeting youth through social media engagement and branded emojis, Maggi has consistently adapted its strategies to remain relevant in the ever-evolving market landscape.

Memorable campaigns like the 'Mood Bana Dost Joda' digital campaign and the #WeMissYouToo campaign during the temporary ban in 2015 have demonstrated Maggi's agility and resilience in maintaining consumer engagement and brand loyalty.

Nestle's "Good Food, Good Life" Campaign

The Nestlé "Good Food, Good Life" campaign stands as one of the company's most ambitious endeavors aimed at promoting a healthy lifestyle and encouraging individuals to make healthier food choices. At the core of this campaign is the idea that consuming Nestlé products can contribute to a balanced and nutritious diet, thereby supporting overall well-being.

One of the key elements of the campaign is its inclusivity, showcasing people from different cultures enjoying Nestlé products as part of their daily routines. By featuring diverse individuals, Nestlé communicates that its products are accessible and relevant to people worldwide, regardless of their background or lifestyle.

Nestlé's marketing campaigns, including "Good Food, Good Life," have been highly successful due to their ability to tell compelling stories that resonate with audiences on a global scale. These campaigns go beyond mere product promotion; they tap into universal themes such as health, happiness, and connection, eliciting emotional responses from viewers.

Through bold storytelling and engaging visuals, Nestlé's marketing campaigns have effectively communicated the brand's values and commitments to consumers. By positioning itself as a company that cares about promoting healthy lifestyles and supporting well-being, Nestlé has strengthened its brand identity and solidified its status as a global leader in the food and beverage industry.

1. **Product Innovation**: Nestlé's approach to product innovation goes beyond introducing new products; it involves pioneering industry-changing innovations that anticipate and shape consumer needs. Their research and development team continuously works to create novel concepts that redefine the culinary landscape, positioning Nestlé at the forefront of the food and beverage industry.
2. **Targeted Marketing**: Nestlé understands the diversity among consumers and tailors its marketing campaigns to speak directly to different segments. By crafting narratives that resonate with specific consumer groups, Nestlé ensures that its messaging aligns with the desires and concerns of each audience, creating a personalized connection with consumers.
3. **Celebrity Endorsements**: Leveraging celebrity endorsements, such as those of Bollywood superstars Shah Rukh Khan and Deepika Padukone, Nestlé adds credibility and charm to its brand. These endorsements not only capture consumer attention but also elevate Nestlé's products from ordinary to extraordinary in the eyes of consumers, boosting brand recognition and appeal.
4. **Social Media Mastery**: Nestlé effectively utilizes social media platforms to engage directly with consumers, fostering conversations, and building relationships. By actively participating in online discussions and promptly responding to inquiries, Nestlé remains attuned to consumer needs and preferences in the digital realm, positioning itself as a brand that values genuine connections.
5. **Co-Branding Collaborations**: Strategic partnerships with industry leaders, such as Starbucks, enable Nestlé to amplify product promotions and expand its product range. These collaborations leverage the combined reputation and customer base of trusted partners, enhancing the consumer experience and showcasing Nestlé's ability to form successful alliances.
6. **Sampling Programs**: Nestlé's sampling programs offer consumers firsthand experience of their products, boosting awareness and generating buzz through word-of-mouth. By providing complimentary product samples, Nestlé forges a connection with consumers that transcends traditional marketing, leaving a lasting impression and fostering brand loyalty.
7. **Strategic Partnerships**: Nestlé strategically partners with other companies to elevate product visibility and reach a wider audience. By teaming up with brands like Coca-Cola, Nestlé creates impactful product launches and sparks consumer interest through collaborative initiatives.
8. **Cause-Related Marketing**: Nestlé engages in cause-related marketing to support noble causes while promoting its products. By aligning with organizations like UNICEF, Nestlé demonstrates its commitment to positive change and fosters a profound connection with consumers who value purpose-driven brands.
9. **Event Sponsorship**: Nestlé sponsors various events to showcase its products and promote healthy living. By aligning its brand with events that celebrate good food and well-being, Nestlé creates meaningful connections with consumers who prioritize health and happiness.
10. **Digital Marketing: The Click and Connect Era**: In the digital age, Nestlé leverages digital channels to create engaging and interactive campaigns that captivate and connect with consumers. From social media to email marketing, Nestlé ensures its presence where the digital conversation is happening, fostering real-time engagement and brand interaction.

Nestle's Secret Weapon: DAT

Nestlé's digital transformation journey offers valuable insights into how companies can adapt to the evolving landscape of digital marketing and leverage technology to stay ahead of the competition. While your company may not have initially prioritized digital transformation, it's never too late to implement a strategy to enhance your digital presence and engagement.

When Nestlé established its Digital Acceleration Team (DAT), it marked a significant shift in the company's focus towards digital marketing. This team was tasked with exploring and leveraging potential advertising technologies to drive innovation and growth in the digital space. The DAT played a pivotal role in training employees across the organization in various aspects of digital marketing, including social media management and search engine optimization (SEO). By empowering employees with digital skills, Nestlé ensured that its workforce was equipped to navigate and capitalize on the digital landscape effectively.

Moreover, the DAT at Nestlé was instrumental in experimenting with novel digital trends and approaches to advertising. By continuously testing and iterating on digital strategies, Nestlé remained at the forefront of digital marketing innovation, allowing the company to stay relevant and maintain a cutting-edge approach to its marketing initiatives. This commitment to experimentation and adaptation enabled Nestlé to cultivate a global brand presence that encompasses thousands of smaller brands under its umbrella.

Crucially, Nestlé invested in a dedicated team of 12 employees tasked with scouting and testing new advertising technologies. These individuals were responsible for staying abreast of emerging digital trends and technologies, as well as evaluating their potential impact on Nestlé's digital footprint. The team leveraged real-time data trends to gain insights into consumer behavior, sentiment, and engagement across digital channels. By monitoring metrics such as trending posts, conversations, and sentiment levels, the DAT could identify opportunities to engage with digital followers effectively and optimize its marketing efforts in real-time.

What We Can Learn from Social Networking at Nestle

Nestlé's approach to social networking encompasses both external and internal platforms, reflecting a comprehensive strategy to leverage the power of social media for both consumer engagement and internal collaboration.

Externally, Nestlé maintains a significant presence across various social media channels, including Facebook, Twitter, and others. With numerous brands featuring their own dedicated pages, Nestlé collectively posts over 1500 times per day, reaching a vast audience of consumers. The company's Facebook pages alone boast more than 180 million fans, indicating the scale and reach of Nestlé's social media footprint. Additionally, Nestlé strategically partners with social media giants like Facebook and Google, enabling it to stay abreast of emerging trends, social technologies, and online advertising opportunities. By forging such partnerships, Nestlé gains valuable insights into consumer behavior and preferences, allowing the company to tailor its marketing efforts effectively.

Internally, Nestlé fosters a culture of collaboration and innovation through a private social network accessible to its employees. This platform serves as a hub for employees to engage with one another, share ideas, and collaborate on various initiatives. With a network spanning 200,000 employees, Nestlé encourages active participation and idea-sharing among its workforce. Employees are incentivized to contribute innovative ideas, which are then evaluated and ranked, fostering a culture of innovation and thought leadership within the organization. This approach not only empowers employees to share their insights and expertise but also cultivates a sense of community and camaraderie within the company.

By embracing both external and internal social networking platforms, Nestlé demonstrates a holistic approach to leveraging social media for business success. Externally, the company engages with consumers, builds brand awareness, and drives marketing initiatives through various social channels. Internally, Nestlé promotes collaboration, creativity, and knowledge-sharing among its employees, fostering a culture of innovation and continuous improvement. This dual approach underscores the importance of social networking in driving both external engagement and internal collaboration, ultimately contributing to Nestlé's overall success in the digital age.

Nestle's Six Points of Brand Building

Nestlé's approach to digital brand building is rooted in a six-point strategy that emphasizes innovation, customer-centricity, shopper engagement, creative experiences, product excellence, and brand inspiration. By focusing on these key pillars, Nestlé aims to leverage digital technologies to enhance its brand presence, engage with customers effectively, and drive business growth.

1. **Innovating**: Nestlé prioritizes innovation in its digital strategy, continually seeking out new technologies and trends to stay ahead of the curve. By embracing innovation, Nestlé can differentiate itself in the competitive marketplace and offer unique experiences to its customers.
2. **Knowing its customers**: Understanding customer preferences, behaviors, and needs is essential for Nestlé to tailor its digital initiatives effectively. Through data analysis and customer insights, Nestlé can create personalized experiences that resonate with its target audience, driving engagement and loyalty.
3. **Winning over shoppers**: Nestlé recognizes the importance of shopper engagement in driving sales and brand loyalty. By leveraging digital channels such as e-commerce platforms and social media, Nestlé can reach shoppers at various touchpoints along their purchasing journey, influencing their buying decisions and driving conversions.
4. **Forming creative and engaging brand experiences**: Nestlé places a strong emphasis on creativity and engagement in its digital branding efforts. By crafting compelling content and interactive experiences, Nestlé can captivate audiences and foster meaningful connections with its brand.
5. **Granting excellent product experience**: Ensuring a seamless and enjoyable product experience is crucial for Nestlé to build trust and loyalty among its customers. By leveraging digital technologies, Nestlé can enhance product visibility, accessibility, and convenience, delivering value to consumers at every interaction point.
6. **Using and inspiring through its brand vision**: Nestlé aligns its digital branding efforts with its brand vision and values, aiming to inspire and resonate with its audience on a deeper level. By communicating a clear brand message and purpose through digital channels, Nestlé can forge emotional connections and build brand affinity.

In addition to its strategic approach to digital brand building, Nestlé also adopts a dynamic marketing approach that blends traditional and digital media channels. By incorporating technologies like QR codes on packaging, Nestlé bridges the gap between traditional and digital marketing, catering to a diverse audience and catering to evolving consumer behaviors. This blended approach allows Nestlé to maintain relevance with both its traditional customer base and younger, tech-savvy demographics.

A complex interplay of consumer preferences, demographic shifts, and socio-economic factors is driving the market demand for healthy products. Increasingly, consumers view diet as a means not only to nourish themselves but also to enhance health, performance, and disease prevention. They seek food products that provide energy, support growth and development, and alleviate health issues, all while offering great taste and convenience.

Changing demographics, particularly the rapid growth of the ageing population, are reshaping the market landscape. With approximately 600 million people worldwide over the age of 60, a number expected to double in the next two decades, there's a growing demand for products that support healthy ageing. As individuals live longer, they aspire to maintain independence and a high quality of life, necessitating nutrition solutions tailored to their evolving needs.

Socio-economic factors further influence market dynamics. The rising prevalence of obesity globally has heightened awareness of the importance of balanced nutrition and physical activity. Consequently, there's a continued demand for products with weight management benefits. Additionally, malnutrition remains a significant concern, prompting the food industry to prioritize fortification efforts to address nutrient deficiencies.

From a public health perspective, proactive nutrition plays a vital role in preventive healthcare, particularly given the increasing prevalence of chronic diseases like diabetes and cardiovascular ailments. Prevention is considered the most effective strategy, especially in regions with strained healthcare systems.

As a leading global food company, Nestlé is committed to promoting health and wellness worldwide, recognizing the evolving nutrition needs of diverse populations. Nestlé's approach aligns with the industry's progression from providing basic sustenance to ensuring taste, convenience, and now, nutrition and wellness. Leveraging its extensive portfolio of over 8000 brands, Nestlé has been actively optimizing the nutritional value of its products over the past five years.

Nestlé's strategic approach to nutrition and wellness encompasses innovation in product development, renovation of existing offerings, and enhanced nutrition assessments in product testing. By staying abreast of scientific and nutritional advancements, Nestlé aims to empower consumers to integrate nutrition and wellness seamlessly into their daily lives through a diverse range of nutritious and enjoyable food products.

Innovations on ingredients deliver health and wellness benefits

Branded active ingredients (BAIs) represent a significant advancement in Nestlé's approach to nutrition, health, and wellness in its products. These substances are physiologically active components that offer health or wellness benefits beyond the basic taste and nutrient content of a product. While the concept of certain foods providing specific health benefits has been recognized for centuries, the formal scientific discovery and exploration of these ingredients began in the 1700s and gained momentum in the late 1800s.

Nestlé has been at the forefront of leveraging BAIs to enhance the health-promoting properties of its products. By isolating and replicating specific ingredients found in natural sources such as plants, Nestlé scientists have developed innovative formulations that can be integrated into a wide range of food and beverage products. For example, the chicory root, a well-known ingredient in human foods, serves as the source of prebiotic inulin, which forms the basis of Nestlé's BAI Prebio1. This ingredient is utilized in powdered milks for toddlers and young children to support digestive health and function.

Nestlé incorporates BAIs into numerous products for both adults and children, including yogurts, milks, beverages, and infant formulas. These products are developed based on scientific research and extensive laboratory trials conducted by Nestlé scientists or in collaboration with universities worldwide. The health claims associated with BAIs in Nestlé products are grounded in scientific evidence, demonstrating the company's commitment to delivering nutritionally sound and beneficial products to consumers.

Continuous renovation leads to healthier products

Nestlé's commitment to product innovation and improvement extends across its diverse product portfolio, with a particular focus on enhancing nutritional quality and health benefits. Over the past five years, Nestlé has undertaken significant efforts to renovate and reformulate its products, resulting in the introduction of over 600 new or improved items in various categories such as water, yogurt, milk, cereal, biscuits, ice cream, and prepared frozen meals.

These improvements encompass a wide range of changes aimed at addressing consumer preferences and nutritional needs. Nestlé has focused on reducing calories, sugars, fats, and salts in its products, as well as offering smaller portion sizes to promote healthier consumption habits. Additionally, the company has fortified its products with essential nutrients such as iron, iodine, vitamins, and minerals to enhance their nutritional value. Moreover, Nestlé has incorporated fruits and whole grains into its formulations to increase fiber content and provide additional health benefits.

Importantly, Nestlé recognizes that indulgent products like confectionery and ice cream also have a place in consumers' diets, even as they prioritize health and wellness. Therefore, the company approaches the renovation of these items with careful consideration for taste and sensory experience. While reducing sugar or calories in indulgent products, Nestlé ensures that taste and quality are not compromised, maintaining the enjoyable aspects that consumers expect from these treats.

By balancing nutritional improvements with consumer preferences for taste and indulgence, Nestlé demonstrates its commitment to providing products that contribute to a balanced diet while meeting consumer expectations for flavor and enjoyment. This approach aligns with Nestlé's overarching goal of promoting health and well-being through its product offerings.

Product labeling takes on new importance with today's consumers

Nestlé recognizes the significant influence that product packaging has on consumers' food choices and acknowledges the opportunity it presents to raise awareness about nutrition and health across diverse demographics. While traditionally, consumers with higher education levels may pay closer attention to product packaging for nutritional information, Nestlé aims to leverage this point of contact to educate all shoppers, regardless of their backgrounds.

To achieve this goal, Nestlé is implementing several strategies to improve the clarity and accessibility of nutritional information on its product packaging. This includes enhancing the overall presentation of nutritional details and providing product labeling, even in regions where it is not mandated by law. By proactively including this information, Nestlé ensures that consumers have access to key nutritional facts to make informed decisions about their food choices.

Moreover, Nestlé is incorporating simple, scientifically-based nutrition messages on its packaging to communicate the health benefits of its products effectively. These messages are designed to be easily understood by a wide range of consumers, promoting transparency and clarity in nutritional communication. Additionally, Nestlé is revising information on preparation methods to offer practical suggestions for healthier cooking practices, such as recommending the use of less oil or substituting salt with herbs and spices.

Through these initiatives, Nestlé aims to empower consumers with the knowledge and tools they need to make healthier food choices. By leveraging product packaging as a platform for education and awareness, Nestlé demonstrates its commitment to promoting health and well-being among consumers worldwide.

Sharing our knowledge and information

Nestlé recognizes the importance of providing consumers with accurate and accessible nutrition-related information. As consumers increasingly seek to make informed choices about their diet and health, Nestlé views this as a reflection of the trust they place in its brands and considers it a responsibility to facilitate their understanding of its products and balanced nutrition principles

To address consumer inquiries and provide support, Nestlé has established Nestlé Online, a telephone helpline available in numerous countries. This service fields hundreds of consumer calls each week, offering assistance and information on various nutrition-related queries. Additionally, Nestlé leverages the power of the internet to engage with consumers interested in nutrition. Through its corporate nutrition website, Nestlé provides a centralized hub for consumers to access comprehensive resources and information on nutrition.

Furthermore, Nestlé tailors its nutrition resources to cater to specific regional and product-related needs. For example, in the UK, Nestlé has developed a "Wellbeing" website aimed at children and their parents, offering insights into topics such as calories and healthy weight management. Similarly, in the US, the Lean Cuisine website features an "Ask the Nutritionist" feature, allowing consumers to seek personalized advice and information on nutrition-related matters.

By offering a range of accessible channels and resources, Nestlé aims to empower consumers to make informed decisions about their diet and nutrition. These initiatives underscore Nestlé's commitment to transparency, consumer education, and promoting healthy lifestyles across diverse demographics and regions.

Nestlé people take charge of the nutrition strategy

Nestlé recognizes that its employees play a crucial role in implementing its nutrition strategy effectively. To ensure seamless integration of the strategy across diverse cultural and operational landscapes, Nestlé has established a team of Nestlé Nutrition Champions. These champions operate within strategic business units and countries, serving as ambassadors for Nestlé's nutrition initiatives. They work closely with experts at product technology centers to ensure alignment with global standards and best practices in nutrition.

The commitment to strengthening employees' knowledge and understanding of nutrition is fundamental to Nestlé's approach. Through various training activities, including interactive e-learning modules and quarterly newsletters on key nutrition topics, Nestlé provides employees, including senior managers, with opportunities to enhance their nutrition literacy. These resources are distributed globally through the company's intranet and other platforms, ensuring widespread access and dissemination of nutrition-related information.

At the corporate level, Nestlé promotes a culture of balanced eating through campaigns such as "Le Plaisir de l'équilibre" (the pleasure of balanced eating), which encourages employees to make nutritious choices for themselves and their families. By fostering an environment that prioritizes nutrition and wellness, Nestlé aligns its internal practices with its external commitments, reinforcing its position as a leader in promoting healthy lifestyles and choices.

Nestlé's relationship with India dates back over a century, commencing in 1912 when it operated as The NESTLÉ Anglo-Swiss Condensed Milk Company (Export) Limited, importing and distributing products in the Indian market. Following India's Independence in 1947, Nestlé responded to the government's focus on local production by establishing a presence in the country. In 1961, Nestlé inaugurated its first factory in Moga, Punjab, aligning with the government's emphasis on developing the milk economy and providing agricultural services to support farmers.

The establishment of milk collection centers in Moga facilitated efficient procurement and fostered community confidence in the dairy industry. Today, Moga thrives as a prosperous milk district, reflecting the success of Nestlé's initiatives. Over the years, Nestlé has become an integral part of India's growth story, providing direct and indirect employment opportunities to approximately one million individuals.

Nestlé India's commitment to understanding evolving lifestyles and anticipating consumer needs drives its operations. Leveraging a culture of innovation and access to the Nestlé Group's technology and expertise, Nestlé India offers a diverse product range focused on Taste, Nutrition, Health, and Wellness. With internationally renowned brands such as NESCAFÉ, MAGGI, MILKYBAR, and others, Nestlé India ensures the delivery of quality products at affordable prices.

Beyond business, Nestlé India is committed to social responsibility, engaging in initiatives to enhance community life. Through its multifaceted approach, Nestlé India embodies corporate excellence and social stewardship, contributing to the nation's progress while nurturing enduring relationships built on trust and integrity.

Nestle India's history dates back to its incorporation in 1959 in New Delhi, promoted by Nestle Alimentana S.A. The company's growth trajectory included strategic initiatives such as fundraising endeavors and expansion efforts. In subsequent decades, Nestle India diversified its product portfolio, entered new segments, and forged strategic alliances to strengthen its market presence.

Amidst market challenges and changing consumer preferences, Nestle India remained agile and responsive, focusing on innovation, sustainability, and social responsibility. Today, Nestle India is a prominent player in the Indian food and beverage industry, reflecting a legacy of resilience, excellence, and commitment to serving consumers and society.

Baby formula Scandal

Nestlé's marketing tactics regarding baby formula have been a source of significant controversy and ethical concern since the 1970s. The company aggressively promoted its infant formula as superior to breast milk, particularly targeting mothers in developing countries in Africa, Latin America, and Asia. Using tactics such as sending saleswomen dressed as nurses to convince mothers, Nestlé perpetuated the false notion that its formula was better for infants than breast milk.

This deceptive marketing strategy had devastating consequences. Many mothers, influenced by Nestlé's marketing and struggling with financial constraints, opted for the formula over breastfeeding. However, due to the high cost of formula and lack of access to clean water and proper sanitation, mothers often diluted the formula with unsanitary water, significantly reducing its nutritional value. As a result, millions of infants suffered malnutrition, and many died as a result of illnesses linked to improper formula preparation.

Despite widespread criticism and condemnation, Nestlé continued to profit from the sale of baby formula. The company's unethical practices, including the failure to educate consumers about proper formula preparation and alleged payments to doctors and hospitals to endorse its products, exacerbated the harm caused to vulnerable populations.

While it's important to acknowledge that some women are unable to breastfeed and that baby formula can serve as a suitable alternative when prepared correctly, Nestlé's exploitation of vulnerable populations for profit is indefensible. Despite decades of global outrage and increased awareness of the harm caused by Nestlé's baby formula, the market for infant formula remains substantial and continues to grow.

This situation underscores the complex interplay between corporate interests, public health, and ethical considerations. It serves as a stark reminder of the importance of corporate accountability and responsible marketing practices, particularly when it comes to products that directly impact the health and well-being of vulnerable populations, such as infants in developing countries.

Backlash Over Unhealthy Food Portfolio

In 2021, Nestlé, the world's largest consumer food and beverage company, faced a significant public backlash following the revelation of an internal presentation highlighting the nutritional shortcomings of a substantial portion of its mainstream product range. According to a report by Hindustan Times, Nestlé disclosed that 60 percent of its food and drinks portfolio, excluding pet food, baby formula, and coffee, did not meet recognized health standards. This admission sparked widespread concern among consumers and health advocates, as it raised questions about the company's commitment to promoting healthy eating habits and providing nutritious options to its customers.

The internal document also acknowledged that certain food products within Nestlé's range might never achieve a healthy status, indicating a systemic issue within the company's product development and marketing practices. This revelation undermined consumer trust in Nestlé's claims regarding the nutritional value of its products and raised doubts about the company's transparency regarding its corporate responsibility practices.

In response to the public scrutiny, Nestlé announced plans to overhaul its nutrition and health strategy and conduct a comprehensive review of its entire product lineup to ensure alignment with nutritional requirements. The company emphasized its efforts to reduce sodium and sugar content across its products by at least 14-15 percent over the past seven years as part of its commitment to promoting healthier choices.

However, despite these assurances, the scandal underscored broader concerns about the food industry's responsibility in addressing public health challenges, such as rising rates of obesity and diet-related diseases. Nestlé's acknowledgment of the nutritional deficiencies in its products highlighted the need for greater transparency and accountability within the food and beverage sector, as well as the importance of regulatory oversight to safeguard consumer interests.

The scandal also prompted a broader conversation about the role of corporations in shaping dietary habits and influencing consumer behavior. Critics argued that companies like Nestlé have a moral obligation to prioritize the health and well-being of their customers over profits and to ensure that their products meet established nutritional standards.

Maggi Noodles Banned in India

The Maggi noodles scandal that unfolded in India between June 2015 and September 2015 had significant repercussions for Nestle India, the manufacturer of the popular instant noodle brand. The controversy began when Sanjay Singh, a food inspector at the Uttar Pradesh government's Food Safety and Drug Administration, discovered irregularities during a routine inspection in March 2014. Singh found packets of Maggi noodles claiming "no added MSG (monosodium glutamate)," prompting him to send a sample for analysis. Subsequent testing revealed the presence of MSG, leading to further examination at the Central Food Laboratory in Kolkata in June 2014. Shockingly, the results, received almost a year later in April 2015, uncovered not only the presence of MSG but also excessive levels of lead, surpassing Nestle India's claims by over 1,000 times.

The findings triggered widespread concern among consumers and health authorities, leading to swift action from regulatory bodies. In May 2015, Nestle issued its first official statement, attempting to reassure consumers about the safety of Maggi noodles. However, the situation escalated when the Food Safety and Standards Authority of India (FSSAI) intervened. On June 5, 2015, the FSSAI ordered Nestle to recall Maggi noodles from the market, citing health hazards posed by the excessive lead content.

The withdrawal of approximately 38,000 tonnes of Maggi noodles from retail shelves across India had a severe impact on Nestle India's operations. Maggi, once the market leader with an 80 percent share, saw its market share plummet to zero practically overnight. The brand's sales accounted for over 25 percent of Nestle India's revenues, making the crisis a significant threat to the company's financial health and reputation in the country.

The fallout from the scandal extended beyond financial losses, tarnishing Nestle's brand image and eroding consumer trust. The incident highlighted the importance of stringent food safety regulations and effective regulatory oversight in ensuring the integrity of food products. It also underscored the need for companies to prioritize transparency and accountability in their operations, particularly in matters concerning public health and safety.

Ultimately, the Maggi noodles scandal served as a cautionary tale for food manufacturers, emphasizing the potential consequences of lapses in quality control and regulatory compliance. It prompted both Nestle India and the Indian government to reassess their food safety protocols and take steps to restore consumer confidence in the aftermath of the crisis.

Boycott in the US for Discouraging Breastfeeding

Nestle's involvement in discouraging breastfeeding in the United States ignited a significant controversy that reverberated both domestically and internationally. Accusations surfaced suggesting that Nestle actively promoted its baby formula as a superior alternative to breastfeeding, despite a lack of substantiated evidence supporting such claims. This marketing strategy raised concerns among health advocates and consumer groups, who argued that it undermined efforts to promote breastfeeding, which is widely recognized as the optimal source of nutrition for infants.

In response to these allegations, a boycott of Nestle products was initiated in the United States in 1977. The boycott gained momentum as consumers and advocacy groups rallied behind the cause, expressing their disapproval of Nestle's marketing practices and its impact on public health. As awareness of the issue grew, the boycott spread to Europe, garnering international attention and amplifying pressure on Nestle to address the controversy.

The boycott persisted for several years, serving as a powerful demonstration of consumer activism and advocacy for breastfeeding rights. During this time, Nestle faced mounting criticism and scrutiny, as the public demanded accountability and transparency regarding its marketing tactics and their potential effects on infant health.

Ultimately, in 1984, Nestle took a significant step towards resolving the crisis by agreeing to adhere to an international marketing code endorsed by the World Health Organization (WHO). This code aimed to regulate the marketing of breast milk substitutes and promote breastfeeding as the preferred method of infant feeding. Nestle's commitment to complying with these guidelines marked a turning point in the controversy and contributed to the official suspension of the boycott in the United States.

The Nestle boycott of the late 1970s and early 1980s underscored the importance of corporate responsibility and ethical marketing practices, particularly in industries that directly impact public health. It served as a catalyst for greater awareness and advocacy surrounding breastfeeding rights and infant nutrition, prompting both companies and regulatory bodies to reevaluate their policies and prioritize the promotion of evidence-based health practices.

Child Slave Labour Accusations

Nestlé's entanglement in legal proceedings over allegations of child slave labor on cocoa farms in the Ivory Coast underscored the complex ethical and humanitarian challenges embedded within global supply chains. The accusations, brought forth by eight former alleged child slaves in 2021, accused Nestlé and other companies of complicity in the illegal enslavement of children working on cocoa farms within their supply chains. These allegations shed light on longstanding concerns regarding the exploitation of vulnerable populations in the production of commodities consumed worldwide.

The lawsuit leveled against Nestlé and other defendants highlighted the immense human toll of such practices, with the petitioners alleging that the companies had facilitated the illegal enslavement of thousands of children on cocoa farms. The case drew attention to the need for heightened scrutiny and accountability throughout complex supply chains, particularly in industries with a history of labor rights abuses and exploitation.

However, in June 2022, a US District Court dismissed the case against Nestlé and other defendants, citing a lack of standing to sue. The court ruled that the plaintiffs failed to establish a "traceable connection" between the defendant companies and the specific plantations where they allegedly worked. This decision underscored the legal complexities inherent in holding multinational corporations accountable for labor practices occurring within their vast and often opaque supply networks.

While the dismissal of the lawsuit may have halted legal proceedings against Nestlé in this instance, the underlying issues of child labor and human rights abuses in cocoa production remain unresolved. The case served as a stark reminder of the need for comprehensive and enforceable mechanisms to address labor rights violations and ensure accountability across global supply chains.

In response to ongoing scrutiny and pressure from stakeholders, including consumers, advocacy groups, and regulatory bodies, companies like Nestlé have taken steps to improve transparency and accountability in their supply chains. However, the persistence of labor rights abuses in industries such as cocoa production underscores the ongoing challenges in eradicating exploitation and ensuring dignity and fair treatment for all workers involved in global commerce.

Exploiting Drought-Ridden Areas

Nestlé's water bottling practices, particularly its operations in drought-prone regions like California, have become a focal point of criticism and controversy. For decades, Nestlé has been extracting water from the San Bernardino National Forest, despite the state's recurring drought conditions. This extraction, which began in 1988, has been a source of contention, especially considering Nestlé's continued usage of the water for its Arrowhead brand since 1984. What exacerbates the situation is that Nestlé has been paying a nominal fee for this water, despite its permit for extraction being expired.

The issue has sparked outrage and led to multiple petitions and legal challenges. Critics argue that Nestlé's extraction practices are unsustainable, particularly in areas facing water scarcity and environmental stress. The fact that Nestlé continues to extract water from the San Bernardino Mountains while paying minimal fees and operating with an expired permit has raised questions about the company's commitment to responsible water stewardship and compliance with regulatory requirements.

In October 2023, the controversy escalated when BlueTriton Brands, Nestlé's subsidiary responsible for its water bottling operations, took legal action against the State Water Resources Control Board's decision to halt "unauthorized diversions" of water from springs in the San Bernardino Mountains. Nestlé argued that the board had exceeded its authority and violated California law by attempting to restrict its water extraction activities. This legal maneuver further intensified public scrutiny and underscored the broader debate surrounding corporate accountability and water resource management.

The Nestlé water bottling scandal in California highlights the complexities and tensions inherent in balancing corporate interests with environmental sustainability and public welfare. As concerns over water scarcity and climate change continue to mount, stakeholders are increasingly calling for greater transparency, accountability, and regulation in the management of water resources, particularly in regions facing acute water stress. The outcome of legal proceedings and ongoing public pressure will likely shape the future of Nestlé's water bottling practices and influence broader discussions about corporate responsibility and environmental conservation.

Among the World's Top Plastic Polluters

Nestlé's packaging practices have come under scrutiny for their contribution to plastic pollution, adding another layer to the ongoing global concern about environmental sustainability. As outlined in a report by Utopia.org, critics have raised significant concerns regarding Nestlé's approach to plastic waste management, particularly highlighting the potential negative impacts of their reliance on incineration as a disposal method. Incineration, critics argue, may not only fail to adequately address the issue of plastic pollution but could also exacerbate it by releasing harmful pollutants into the environment.

Amid growing public pressure and increased awareness of the environmental consequences of plastic waste, Nestlé has made commitments to address the issue. The company's website states its aim for over 95 percent of its plastic packaging to be designed for recycling by 2025, signaling an acknowledgment of the need for action to reduce plastic waste and promote a more sustainable approach to packaging.

However, accusations from organizations like Greenpeace suggest that Nestlé's actions may not align with its stated commitments. Greenpeace alleged that Nestlé was burning its plastic waste, leading to toxic pollution and contradicting the company's purported efforts to increase recycling rates. This dissonance between Nestlé's stated goals and its alleged practices has intensified public scrutiny and raised questions about the company's commitment to environmental stewardship.

The controversy surrounding Nestlé's packaging practices underscores the broader challenges faced by corporations in addressing plastic pollution and promoting sustainability throughout their supply chains. While commitments to recycling and waste reduction are important steps, they must be accompanied by concrete actions and transparent accountability mechanisms to ensure meaningful progress. The discrepancy between Nestlé's aspirations and the reality of its practices highlights the need for greater transparency, oversight, and public engagement to drive meaningful change in addressing the global plastic pollution crisis.

As stakeholders continue to demand accountability and action on environmental issues, including plastic waste management, Nestlé and other corporations face increasing pressure to align their practices with sustainability goals and demonstrate genuine commitment to protecting the planet for future generations. The resolution of this scandal will likely depend on Nestlé's willingness to address the concerns raised by critics and take decisive action to mitigate its environmental impact.

Contaminating Groundwater

Accusations against Nestlé for groundwater exploitation in Pakistan have brought to light significant concerns regarding the company's environmental practices and their impact on local communities. In a country where water scarcity is a pressing issue, Nestlé's operations have allegedly exacerbated the problem, leading to sinking water levels and contamination in affected areas. These allegations have sparked public outrage and raised questions about Nestlé's responsibility in managing and preserving water resources in regions facing acute water stress.

Forensic audits submitted to the Pakistan Supreme Court have revealed troubling findings regarding Nestlé's water management practices. Despite management assertions regarding water wastage during the Reverse Osmosis (RO) process in water treatment, forensic audits have shown significant discrepancies. The audits found that while Nestlé Pakistan acknowledged a 15 percent water wastage rate during RO treatment, they were unable to justify the remaining 28 percent wastage of water, indicating potential inefficiencies or mismanagement in water usage.

Furthermore, allegations suggest that Nestlé may not have fulfilled its financial obligations for the water supply in Pakistan. According to the Business and Human Rights Resource Centre, there are claims that Nestlé made no payments for the water supply, raising concerns about the company's compliance with regulatory requirements and its commitment to ethical business practices.

The scandal surrounding Nestlé's groundwater exploitation in Pakistan underscores broader issues related to corporate accountability, environmental sustainability, and human rights. As communities grapple with the consequences of water scarcity and environmental degradation, multinational corporations like Nestlé have a responsibility to operate in a manner that respects local ecosystems, communities, and regulatory frameworks.

The allegations against Nestlé highlight the urgent need for greater transparency, oversight, and accountability in corporate water management practices. It is imperative for Nestlé to address these allegations seriously, engage with stakeholders, and take concrete actions to mitigate its environmental impact and uphold its commitments to responsible water stewardship.

Ultimately, the resolution of this scandal will depend on Nestlé's willingness to acknowledge its shortcomings, implement corrective measures, and engage in meaningful dialogue with affected communities and regulatory authorities. By prioritizing sustainability, ethical conduct, and stakeholder engagement, Nestlé can work towards rebuilding trust and contributing to positive environmental outcomes in Pakistan and beyond.

Nestlé, as a global leader in the food and beverage industry, recognizes the urgent need to address environmental challenges. With a commitment to sustainability deeply ingrained in its corporate ethos, Nestlé has embarked on a comprehensive journey towards achieving zero environmental impact in its operations by 2030.

One of the cornerstones of Nestlé's sustainability strategy is its focus on renewable energy. The company is actively transitioning towards using 100% renewable electricity by the year 2030. As a member of the RE100 initiative, Nestlé is committed to sourcing its energy needs from renewable sources such as wind, solar, and hydroelectric power. This transition is not only aimed at reducing Nestlé's carbon footprint but also at promoting the adoption of clean energy solutions on a global scale.

Innovative approaches to energy procurement further exemplify Nestlé's commitment to sustainability. For instance, Nestlé has implemented strategies to utilize waste materials as alternative fuel sources in its operations. Coffee grounds and dairy farm manure, which would otherwise be disposed of as waste, are repurposed to generate energy. By embracing this circular economy model, Nestlé not only minimizes waste but also reduces greenhouse gas emissions, contributing to climate change mitigation efforts.

Another key aspect of Nestlé's sustainability agenda is its focus on packaging sustainability. The company has set ambitious targets to make all its packaging 100% recyclable and reusable by 2025. To achieve this goal, Nestlé is investing in research and development to explore innovative packaging materials and design solutions. The Nestlé Institute of Packaging Sciences plays a pivotal role in this endeavor, conducting research to assess the functionality and safety of packaging materials. Additionally, Nestlé is exploring packaging-free alternatives and investing in the use of recycled, biodegradable, and compostable materials to minimize its environmental impact.

Nestlé is also committed to reducing single-use packaging through the introduction of reusable and refillable dispensers for products such as pet food and coffee. Collaborative initiatives with organizations like TerraCycle further underscore Nestlé's dedication to promoting a circular economy and minimizing plastic waste.

Water stewardship is another critical area of focus for Nestlé. The company has set targets to ensure responsible water management across its operations. This includes efforts to reduce water consumption, replenish water sources, and achieve certification under the Alliance for Water Stewardship standard. Technologies such as Aquassay are being implemented to monitor water usage from source to discharge, enabling Nestlé to track and optimize its water footprint.

Furthermore, Nestlé is actively engaged in promoting sustainable agriculture. Through its plant science teams, the company invests in research and development to identify high-performing crop varieties with reduced environmental footprints. By partnering with farmers and providing them with sustainable agricultural practices and technologies, Nestlé aims to enhance agricultural productivity while minimizing environmental impact.

Nestlé's Sustainability Strategy

Nestlé, as a global food and beverage company, has formulated an overarching sustainability strategy that encompasses its commitment to people, the planet, and its products. This chapter delves into Nestlé's three pillars of sustainability and explores the initiatives and practices it has adopted to drive positive change.

<u>People:</u>

Nestlé strongly emphasizes improving the quality of life for individuals and communities. The company recognizes that its success is intertwined with the well-being of its employees and society. Nestlé promotes diversity, inclusion, and equal opportunities within its workforce, fostering a culture of respect and collaboration. Additionally, Nestlé extends its support beyond its employees by partnering with farmers, suppliers, and other stakeholders to ensure fair and responsible practices throughout the value chain.

<u>Planet:</u>

Nestlé is committed to reducing its environmental impact and preserving natural resources. To achieve this, the company has implemented sustainable sourcing practices for its raw materials, working closely with farmers and suppliers to promote responsible agriculture and protect ecosystems. Nestlé also focuses on minimizing waste generation, promoting recycling, and reducing greenhouse gas emissions. Through efficient water management and energy conservation, Nestlé aims to mitigate its ecological footprint and contribute to a more sustainable planet.

<u>Products:</u>

Nestlé recognizes the importance of developing healthier and more sustainable product offerings. The company prioritizes nutrition, portion control, and responsible marketing practices to promote healthier lifestyles and address public health concerns. Nestlé continually innovates to meet consumer demands for sustainable products, exploring ways to reduce sugar, salt, and artificial ingredients in its offerings. Moreover, Nestlé is dedicated to promoting sustainable packaging solutions and responsible disposal methods, aiming to minimize the environmental impact of its products throughout their life cycle.

By focusing on these three pillars, Nestlé's sustainability strategy encompasses a comprehensive approach to address the social, environmental, and economic aspects of its business. Through its commitment to people, planet, and products, Nestlé aims to create shared value for all stakeholders and contribute to a more sustainable future.

Nestlé's sustainability strategy is an ever-evolving journey, with ongoing efforts to continuously improve and adapt to emerging challenges. The company's commitment to transparency and accountability ensures its sustainability initiatives are measurable and aligned with global sustainability goals.

As we explore Nestlé's sustainability journey, let us delve deeper into the specific initiatives and projects that showcase Nestlé's dedication to creating a positive impact and driving sustainable change in the food and beverage industry.

Key Milestones in Nestlé's Sustainability Journey

Nestlé's sustainability journey has been marked by significant achievements and milestones, demonstrating the company's unwavering commitment to driving positive change. This chapter explores key accomplishments in water usage reduction, sustainable agriculture, climate action, and packaging innovation.

Reduction of Water Usage:

Nestlé has integrated a range of water-saving technologies and strategies across its operations, resulting in substantial reductions in its water footprint. Through these efforts, the company has demonstrated its commitment to sustainable water management practices. Additionally, Nestlé actively engages with local communities and stakeholders to foster partnerships aimed at supporting water resource management initiatives. This collaborative approach helps safeguard and conserve water resources for the benefit of present and future generations, reflecting Nestlé's dedication to environmental sustainability and corporate responsibility.

Sustainable Agriculture:

Nestlé acknowledges the critical role of sustainable agriculture in securing the resilience and longevity of its supply chain. Recognizing this, the company actively collaborates with farmers to facilitate the adoption of sustainable agricultural practices aimed at enhancing soil health, preserving biodiversity, and promoting responsible land management. By providing support and resources to farmers, Nestlé empowers them to implement practices that not only benefit their own operations but also contribute to broader environmental conservation efforts.

Furthermore, Nestlé's commitment to sustainable agriculture is underscored by its investments in research and development. Through ongoing R&D initiatives, the company explores and implements innovative farming methods designed to minimize environmental impact while ensuring the quality and safety of raw materials. These efforts enable Nestlé to stay at the forefront of sustainable agricultural practices, continually refining its approach to align with evolving environmental and social considerations.

By prioritizing sustainable agriculture, Nestlé not only strengthens the resilience of its supply chain but also upholds its commitment to environmental stewardship and corporate responsibility. Through collaboration with farmers and investments in R&D, Nestlé demonstrates its dedication to promoting sustainable food production practices that benefit both people and the planet.

Climate Action:

Nestlé has made combating climate change a priority and has undertaken substantial measures to reduce its greenhouse gas emissions. One key aspect of its strategy involves the implementation of energy-efficient technologies throughout its operations. By adopting these technologies, Nestlé aims to minimize energy consumption and reduce emissions associated with its production processes.

In addition to energy efficiency measures, Nestlé has transitioned to renewable energy sources wherever feasible. This shift towards renewable energy helps the company reduce its reliance on fossil fuels, thereby lowering its carbon footprint and contributing to a more sustainable energy future.

Furthermore, Nestlé has optimized its logistics operations to minimize emissions associated with transportation and distribution. This includes efforts to optimize routes, reduce vehicle emissions, and improve fuel efficiency in its transportation fleet.

Nestlé also actively seeks partnerships and collaborations with other organizations, governments, and stakeholders to drive climate action. By working together with like-minded entities, Nestlé can leverage collective expertise, resources, and influence to accelerate progress towards common climate goals. These partnerships enable Nestlé to amplify its impact and contribute to broader global efforts aimed at mitigating the effects of climate change.

Packaging Innovation:

Recognizing the environmental impact of packaging waste, Nestlé has made significant progress in developing sustainable packaging solutions. The company prioritizes the creation of recyclable and biodegradable packaging materials, aiming to reduce reliance on single-use plastics. Through collaboration with industry partners, Nestlé actively explores innovative packaging technologies, with the goal of driving positive change and fostering a circular economy in the food and beverage sector.

Nestlé's sustainability journey is characterized by its dedication to continuous improvement. Understanding that sustainability is an ongoing process that requires constant innovation and adaptation, Nestlé sets ambitious targets and regularly evaluates its progress. The company consistently seeks new opportunities to enhance its environmental performance, demonstrating a commitment to a more sustainable future.

By achieving milestones in water usage reduction, sustainable agriculture, climate action, and packaging innovation, Nestlé sets a precedent for the industry. The company showcases that sustainable practices can be seamlessly integrated into the core operations of a global food and beverage enterprise. As Nestlé continues its sustainability journey, it remains steadfast in pursuing innovative solutions, collaborating with stakeholders, and striving for excellence in environmental stewardship.

The forthcoming chapter will delve into specific initiatives and programs, illustrating Nestlé's steadfast commitment to sustainability and the measures taken to address key environmental challenges in the food and beverage sector.

Nestlé's Collaboration and Partnerships:

Nestlé recognizes that achieving its sustainability goals necessitates collaboration and partnerships with external organizations. This chapter delves into Nestlé's collaborative efforts and partnerships that have played a vital role in advancing its sustainability agenda, focusing particularly on responsible sourcing, waste management, and community development.

In the realm of responsible sourcing, Nestlé has forged partnerships with suppliers, farmers, and industry organizations to promote sustainable agricultural practices and ethical sourcing standards. By working closely with these stakeholders, Nestlé aims to ensure the responsible production of raw materials, minimize environmental impact, and uphold social welfare standards throughout its supply chain.

Additionally, Nestlé collaborates with waste management organizations, recycling initiatives, and packaging suppliers to develop innovative solutions for reducing packaging waste and promoting circular economy principles. Through these partnerships, Nestlé strives to minimize its environmental footprint, increase recycling rates, and mitigate the impacts of packaging waste on ecosystems and communities.

Furthermore, Nestlé engages in partnerships with local communities, non-profit organizations, and government agencies to support community development initiatives. These collaborations focus on areas such as education, healthcare, and economic empowerment, aiming to improve the well-being and livelihoods of communities where Nestlé operates.

<u>Responsible Sourcing:</u>

Nestlé's commitment to responsible sourcing practices is evident through its strategic partnerships with various stakeholders across its supply chain. By collaborating with organizations such as the Rainforest Alliance, Fairtrade International, and the Roundtable on Sustainable Palm Oil (RSPO), Nestlé aims to promote sustainable agricultural practices, protect biodiversity, and support the livelihoods of farmers.

One of Nestlé's key partnerships is with the Rainforest Alliance, a leading non-profit organization focused on conserving biodiversity and promoting sustainable livelihoods. Through this partnership, Nestlé works with farmers to implement sustainable farming practices that prioritize environmental conservation while improving agricultural productivity and livelihoods. The Rainforest Alliance certification program ensures compliance with rigorous sustainability standards, providing consumers with assurance that Nestlé's products are sourced responsibly.

Similarly, Nestlé collaborates with Fairtrade International to promote fair and ethical trade practices, particularly in developing countries. Through Fairtrade certification, Nestlé ensures that farmers receive fair prices for their products, enabling them to invest in their communities and improve their standard of living. This partnership underscores Nestlé's commitment to social responsibility and ethical sourcing.

Additionally, Nestlé is actively involved in the Roundtable on Sustainable Palm Oil (RSPO), a multi-stakeholder initiative aimed at promoting sustainable palm oil production. By partnering with the RSPO, Nestlé works to address the environmental and social challenges associated with palm oil cultivation, including deforestation, habitat loss, and human rights abuses. Through its membership in the RSPO, Nestlé demonstrates its commitment to sourcing palm oil responsibly and supporting the transition to sustainable practices in the palm oil industry.

<u>Waste Management:</u>

Addressing the global challenge of waste management necessitates collaborative efforts involving various stakeholders, and Nestlé is actively engaged in partnerships with governments, NGOs, and industry partners to develop innovative solutions. By leveraging collective expertise and resources, Nestlé seeks to minimize waste generation and promote circular economy principles.

One key collaboration for Nestlé is with organizations like the Ellen MacArthur Foundation, which is dedicated to accelerating the transition towards a circular economy. Through this partnership, Nestlé focuses on rethinking packaging design to optimize recyclability and minimize environmental impact. By incorporating circular economy principles into its packaging strategies, Nestlé aims to reduce the use of single-use plastics and promote the use of sustainable materials.

Furthermore, Nestlé collaborates with governments and NGOs to implement recycling initiatives and improve waste management infrastructure. By supporting programs that encourage recycling and proper waste disposal, Nestlé aims to minimize the environmental impact of its operations and contribute to a more sustainable future.

These partnerships enable Nestlé to play a proactive role in global efforts to address waste management challenges. By working collaboratively with stakeholders across sectors, Nestlé can harness collective knowledge and resources to develop and implement effective solutions. Through its commitment to promoting sustainable waste management practices, Nestlé demonstrates its dedication to environmental stewardship and corporate responsibility.

Community Development:

Nestlé acknowledges the significance of involving and aiding local communities in its sustainability endeavors. The company partners with community-based organizations, NGOs, and governmental bodies to initiate community development projects. Through initiatives like the Nestlé Cocoa Plan and the Nescafé Plan, Nestlé collaborates with farmers and communities to enhance livelihoods, offer education and training, and advocate sustainable agricultural practices. These partnerships empower local communities, improve social welfare, and enhance the overall sustainability of Nestlé's supply chain.

These instances of Nestlé's collaborations and partnerships exemplify the company's dedication to collaborating with external stakeholders to instigate positive transformations. By leveraging collective expertise, resources, and knowledge, Nestlé broadens the scope and impact of its sustainability initiatives. These partnerships enable Nestlé to align its sustainability objectives with global endeavors, stimulate innovation, and generate mutual value throughout the value chain.

Looking ahead, Nestlé remains committed to nurturing strategic partnerships, seeking fresh collaborations, and propelling collective action to confront intricate sustainability challenges. By cooperating closely with external entities, Nestlé aims to cultivate a more sustainable and inclusive future where the principles of responsible sourcing, waste management, and community development are integrated into every facet of its operations.

Impact Measurement and Reporting:

Nestlé places significant emphasis on measuring and reporting its sustainability performance to uphold transparency, accountability, and facilitate continuous improvement. This chapter delves into Nestlé's methodology for impact measurement and reporting, underscoring the company's dedication to communicating progress, addressing challenges, and setting future targets.

By systematically evaluating its sustainability efforts, Nestlé ensures transparency in its operations and demonstrates accountability to stakeholders. Through comprehensive reporting, Nestlé provides insights into its environmental, social, and governance practices, allowing stakeholders to assess the company's performance and contributions towards sustainability goals.

Moreover, Nestlé's commitment to continuous improvement is reflected in its approach to impact measurement and reporting. By regularly monitoring key performance indicators and benchmarks, Nestlé identifies areas for enhancement and implements strategies to drive positive change. Through transparent reporting of progress, Nestlé fosters a culture of accountability and encourages stakeholder engagement in sustainability initiatives.

Measuring Sustainability Performance:

Nestlé employs a robust framework to measure its sustainability performance across various dimensions. The company utilizes key performance indicators (KPIs) aligned with its sustainability goals and international standards, such as the Global Reporting Initiative (GRI) and the Sustainability Accounting Standards Board (SASB). By tracking and analyzing data related to water usage, greenhouse gas emissions, waste management, and other relevant metrics, Nestlé gains insights into its environmental and social impact.

Reporting Progress:

Transparency lies at the core of Nestlé's sustainability endeavors, and the company demonstrates this commitment through the publication of annual sustainability reports. These reports serve as vital resources, offering detailed insights into Nestlé's progress, initiatives, and challenges in the realm of sustainability. By providing comprehensive information on various aspects of its sustainability efforts, Nestlé aims to foster transparency and accountability.

In these reports, Nestlé articulates its sustainability strategy, delineating its approach to addressing key environmental, social, and governance issues. The reports showcase the company's commitment to sustainability goals and outline the strategies and actions undertaken to achieve them. By transparently sharing its sustainability strategy, Nestlé seeks to build trust with stakeholders and demonstrate its dedication to responsible business practices.

Moreover, Nestlé's sustainability reports go beyond mere rhetoric by presenting tangible achievements and outcomes resulting from its sustainability initiatives. Through data-driven insights and performance indicators, Nestlé offers concrete evidence of progress made towards its sustainability objectives. This transparency enables stakeholders to assess Nestlé's performance objectively and hold the company accountable for its actions.

Crucially, Nestlé's adherence to recognized reporting frameworks, such as the Global Reporting Initiative (GRI) Standards, further enhances the credibility and comparability of the information presented in its sustainability reports. By aligning with established reporting standards, Nestlé ensures that its sustainability disclosures are consistent, transparent, and reliable, enabling stakeholders to make informed decisions and comparisons.

Sharing Challenges and Future Targets:

Nestlé openly acknowledges that sustainability is an ongoing journey fraught with challenges. In its reporting, the company candidly addresses these challenges, underscoring its commitment to transparency and willingness to learn from past experiences. Additionally, Nestlé sets ambitious targets for the future, outlining its commitments and plans to drive further improvements. By sharing both challenges and future targets, Nestlé invites stakeholders to participate in its efforts and holds itself accountable for progress.

Moreover, Nestlé's approach to impact measurement and reporting transcends mere compliance with reporting requirements. The company aims to foster transparency, engage stakeholders, and catalyze positive change within both the company and the wider industry. By effectively measuring and reporting its sustainability performance, Nestlé enhances trust, builds credibility, and facilitates informed decision-making among stakeholders.

1. **Baby Formula Scandal:** Nestlé's involvement in unethical marketing practices regarding baby formula raised serious concerns about its commitment to public health and corporate responsibility. In response, Nestlé has strengthened its focus on responsible marketing practices, particularly concerning infant nutrition. The company has worked to adhere to international guidelines, such as the *WHO Code*, to regulate the marketing of breast milk substitutes. Additionally, Nestlé has invested in *education and support programs* for breastfeeding mothers, aiming to promote breastfeeding as the optimal choice while ensuring access to safe and nutritious infant formula for those who need it.

2. **Backlash Over Unhealthy Food Portfolio:** Nestlé faced criticism over the nutritional shortcomings of its food and beverage products. To address this, Nestlé has committed to overhauling its nutrition and health strategy, aiming to align its product portfolio with recognized health standards. The company has focused on *reducing sodium and sugar content* across its products and has pledged to review its entire product lineup to prioritize healthier options. By taking these steps, Nestlé aims to regain consumer trust and demonstrate its commitment to promoting healthier eating habits.

3. **Maggi Noodles Scandal:** The controversy surrounding Maggi noodles highlighted concerns about food safety and quality control. Nestlé India responded by implementing *stringent quality assurance measures* and revamping its production processes to ensure compliance with food safety standards. The company has also engaged in extensive communication and transparency efforts to rebuild consumer confidence in the safety and integrity of its products.

4. **Child Slave Labour Accusations:** Allegations of child slave labor in Nestlé's cocoa supply chain underscored the need for improved transparency and accountability in supply chain management. Nestlé has since taken steps to address these issues, such as implementing comprehensive due diligence processes to identify and mitigate the risk of child labor in its supply chains. The company has also *collaborated with industry partners, NGOs, and governments* to tackle child labor and improve working conditions in cocoa-producing regions.

5. **Exploiting Drought-Ridden Areas:** Nestlé's water bottling practices in drought-prone regions have faced scrutiny for their impact on water resources and the environment. In response, Nestlé has committed to responsible *water stewardship* by implementing water-saving measures in its operations and engaging with stakeholders to address concerns about water extraction. The company has also invested in community water projects to support sustainable water management practices in affected areas.

6. **Among the World's Top Plastic Polluters:** Nestlé has faced criticism for its contribution to plastic pollution through its packaging practices. In response, Nestlé has set ambitious targets to make its packaging more sustainable, *aiming for over 95% of its plastic packaging to be recyclable or reusable by 2025*. The company has also invested in research and development to explore alternative packaging materials and recycling technologies, demonstrating its commitment to reducing plastic waste and promoting a circular economy.

7. **Contaminating Groundwater:** Allegations of groundwater exploitation in Pakistan have prompted Nestlé to reassess its water management practices and engage with stakeholders to address concerns. The company has conducted *audits* to evaluate its water usage and has pledged to improve efficiency and transparency in water management. Nestlé has also committed to fulfilling its financial obligations for water supply and supporting initiatives to protect and preserve water resources in affected areas.

References

1. Pereira, D. (2023, April 13). *Nestlé Swot Analysis (2024)*. Business Model Analyst. https://businessmodelanalyst.com/nestle-swot-analysis/
2. Team, M. S. (2023, June 29). *Nestle Pestle analysis - detailed Pestel factors*. https://www.mbaskool.com/pestle-analysis/companies/17962-nestle.html
3. Admin. (2024, January 18). *Nestle Pestel Analysis - The Strategy Story*. The Strategy Story - Simplifying Business Strategies. https://thestrategystory.com/blog/nestle-pestel-analysis/
4. Frue, K. (2024, March 25). *Pest analysis of Nestle: How Politics and Social Culture affect its growth*. PESTLE Analysis. https://pestleanalysis.com/pest-analysis-of-nestle/
5. *The Pest Analysis of Nestle*. Bartleby. (n.d.). https://www.bartleby.com/essay/The-Pest-Analysis-Of-Nestle-PCVHY6TE26
6. Xaif. (2023a, October 27). *Complete marketing mix of Nestle with 4PS in detail*. IIDE. https://iide.co/case-studies/marketing-mix-of-nestle/
7. *Nestlé Marketing Mix (4PS) analysis*. Boardmix. (n.d.). https://boardmix.com/analysis/nestle-marketing-mix/
8. Bhasin, H. (2024, January 20). *Marketing mix of Nestle and 4PS (updated 2023)*. Marketing91. https://www.marketing91.com/marketing-mix-nestle/
9. Dan. (2024, April 1). *Successful Marketing Strategies of Nestle (with campaign examples)*. Digital Agency Network. https://digitalagencynetwork.com/successful-marketing-strategies-of-nestle-for-your-inspiration/
10. Simplilearn. (2023, October 30). *10 key takeaways from the nestle marketing strategy: Simplilearn*. Simplilearn.com. https://www.simplilearn.com/tutorials/marketing-case-studies-tutorial/key-takeaways-from-nestle-marketing-strategy
11. Karthikeyan, A. (2023, May 5). *Nestle's Marketing Strategies: Building Trust, boosting sales*. StartupTalky. https://startuptalky.com/nestle-marketing-strategies/
12. Productions, T. E. B. (2023, October 6). *Nestle's marketing strategy [2023]:* End to End Media Solutions Company in Mumbai India | Third Eye Blind Productions. https://thirdeyeblindproductions.com/nestles-marketing-strategy/
13. Productions, T. E. B. (2023a, October 6). *Nestle's marketing strategy [2023]:* End to End Media Solutions Company in Mumbai India | Third Eye Blind Productions. https://thirdeyeblindproductions.com/nestles-marketing-strategy/
14. *Business studies*. StudySmarter UK. (n.d.). https://www.studysmarter.co.uk/explanations/business-studies/business-case-studies/pricing-strategy-of-nestle-company/
15. Admin. (2023, September 28). *Nestle Case Study: How Nestle's marketing strategy helped them grow -2023*. Streamlyn Academy. https://streamlynacademy.com/blog/nestle-case-study/
16. Case study of NESTLÉ1. (n.d.). https://accid.org/wp-content/uploads/2019/09/CASE-NESTLEformatv.pdf
17. *Strategic-management-case-study-analysis-of-nestle (PDF)*. CliffsNotes. (n.d.). https://www.cliffsnotes.com/study-notes/1643986
18. Sustainability, M. (2023, July 10). *From vision to action: Unraveling nestlé's Sustainability Journey and Environmental pledge*. LinkedIn. https://www.linkedin.com/pulse/from-vision-action-unraveling-nestl%C3%A9s-sustainability/
19. *Case study- Nestle*. ICCE: Circular Economy. (2021a, September 1). https://ic-ce.com/case-study-nestle/
20. *Nestlé ad campaigns*. Nestlé. (n.d.). https://www.nestle.in/brands/tvc
21. *Nestle Mission and Vision Statement Analysis*. Edrawsoft. (n.d.). https://www.edrawmind.com/article/nestle-mission-and-vision-statement-analysis.html
22. *About Us*. Nestlé. (n.d.-a). https://www.nestle.in/aboutus
23. Slideshare. (2016, April 22). *Nestle - Brand Management*. SlideShare. https://www.slideshare.net/ShannonCavanaghEdwar/nestle-brand-management

24. Moneycontrol.com. (n.d.). *Nestle India > Company History > Food Processing > company history of Nestle India - BSE: 500790, NSE: Nestleind*. English. https://www.moneycontrol.com/company-facts/nestleindia/history/NI

25. Marketing Week. (2014, October 1). *Nestlé acts to boost its corporate image*. https://www.marketingweek.com/nestle-acts-to-boost-its-corporate-image/

26. *Sustainability at nestlé*. Nestlé Global. (n.d.). https://www.nestle.com/sustainability?__cf_chl_tk=FrBD0mQEL8nentaVTB1D7kVjnbEPlm4PID Y7nGQhfZA-1714317341-0.0.1.1-1493

27. News - kantar worldpanel. (n.d.). https://www.kantarworldpanel.com/global/News/Case-study-Nestle-Innovation-for-untapped-consumption-occasions3

28. *Nestle's major controversies in India and globally: From adding sugar in baby food to maggi ban*. Hindustan Times. (2024, April 18). https://www.hindustantimes.com/business/nestles-top-controversies-in-india-and-globally-from-adding-sugar-in-baby-food-to-maggi-ban-101713421205235.html

29. *Case studies*. Nestlé. (n.d.). https://www.nestle.pk/csvnestle/casestudies?__cf_chl_rt_tk=EoNhp3uNS19R6Dsm1Y.jGrFnOnZg k7ARSLpK2ZemX6g-1714318079-0.0.1.1-1514